SERMON PREPARATION

SERMON
PREPARATION

BILL HYBELS
TIMOTHY KELLER
JEFFREY ARTHURS
MARK DRISCOLL
KENT HUGHES
DAVE STONE
SCOTT WENIG
And more...

Craig Brian Larson, General Editor

Sermon Preparation

Hendrickson Publishers Marketing, LLC
P. O. Box 3473
Peabody, Massachusetts 01961-3473

ISBN 978-1-59856-960-5

Printed in the United States of America

First Hendrickson Edition Printing — August 2012

Library of Congress Cataloging-in-Publication Data

Sermon preparation.
     p. cm. — (The preacher's toolbox ; bk. 4)
     ISBN 978-1-59856-960-5 (alk. paper)
     1. Preaching.
     BV4211.3.S47 2012
     251′.01—dc23
                      2012017818

TABLE OF CONTENTS

Part Two—How I Prepare a Sermon: Interviews

FOREWORD

"Wisdom is supreme; therefore get wisdom.
Though it cost all you have, get understanding."
(Proverbs 4:7)

That verse certainly applies to preaching. As editor of PreachingToday.com since 1999, I have listened to many sermons, and it is sobering to consider how many ways preaching can go wrong, from bad theology to bad interpretation of texts, from extremes on one side to extremes on the other, from being a people pleaser to being a people abuser, from confusing hearers to boring them. If there is any group of people in dire need of wisdom, it is preachers.

We find that wisdom in Scripture in large measure, of course. But while the Bible is our all-sufficient source book for what we preach, and for the theology of preaching and the character of the preacher, it is not a preaching manual. For much of what we need to know about preaching in our generation, in our geography, we need wisdom from one another.

We need the insights of those who have preached for fifty years, who have seen fads come and go, who have made mistakes themselves, and who can keep us from repeating them. We need the new perspective of young preachers who understand where the culture is going in ways that veteran preachers may not.

We need to hear from contemporary preachers who have read the wisdom of the church collected over hundreds of years on the subjects of preaching, pastoring, the care of the soul, theology, interpretation, sermon application, human nature, communication. We need to hear the wisdom of other "tribes" within the church, for each denomination or movement develops its own way of preaching, with its particular strengths and weaknesses.

In this book series, you will find a breadth of such wisdom. Since 1999 PreachingToday.com has published articles each month from outstanding practitioners on the essentials of preaching. This series of books with Hendrickson will draw from that bank vault of wisdom, bringing you timeless wisdom for contemporary preaching with the goal of equipping you for the most important work in the world, the proclamation of the glorious gospel of our Lord Jesus Christ.

And week by week, through the ups and downs, ins and outs of their lives, your congregation will be glad they have come to the house of the Lord to hear you preach. In your voice, your flock will hear the voice of the chief Shepherd, the Overseer of their souls.

Let it be, O Lord, by your grace!

—Craig Brian Larson, editor of PreachingToday.com

Preparing Your Heart and Honing Your Skills

FIVE HAMMER STROKES FOR CREATING EXPOSITORY SERMON OUTLINES

Here are the fundamentals to move from a biblical text to a message structure that speaks to today's listeners.

Jeffrey Arthurs

Martyn Lloyd-Jones, a great preacher of London in the mid-twentieth century, knew that structuring the sermon is one of our most difficult homiletical tasks:

> The preparation of sermons involves sweat and labour. It can be extremely difficult at times to get all this matter that you have found in the Scriptures into [an outline]. It is like a . . . blacksmith making shoes for a horse; you have to keep on putting the material into the fire and on to the anvil and hit it again and again with the hammer. Each time it is a bit better, but not quite right; so you put it back again and again until you are satisfied with it or can do no better. This is the most grueling part of the preparation of a sermon; but at

the same time it is a most fascinating and a most glorious occupation. (*Preachers and Preaching*, 80)

This article can't (and shouldn't) stop the sweat and labor, but it can help you strike skillfully. When pastors begin their sermon prep (and, unfortunately, sometimes when they *end* their sermon prep), the text often seems to be, as Hamlet said, "words, words, words." The relationships among the words—the *ideas* presented—are hard to discern and even harder to package for the congregation. The purpose of this article is to help us make sense of the words and structure them in a way that makes sense to the listeners. As homiletical blacksmiths, five strokes of the hammer help us structure our sermons.

First stroke: state the exegetical outline

Summarize the flow of thought in your text. We call this the exegetical outline, and it is part of basic exegesis. If you have gotten away from that discipline, get back to it. Charting the flow of thought with a mechanical layout, grammatical diagram, or semantic structural analysis is an indispensible step in creating an expository sermon. Simply identifying a general theme is not enough to reveal authorial intention. Laying out the major ideas and their relationships will help you identify the unifying core of the text, what Haddon Robinson calls the exegetical idea.

Once you articulate that idea, then you can turn it into your sermon's "big idea." In essay writing this is called the thesis. In public speaking it is called the central idea. The big idea is the distilled essence of the message. Compare the exegetical idea (the text's central truth) and the big idea (the sermon's central truth):

Exegetical idea	Big idea
Purpose—to summarize the passage in a single sentence	Purpose—to communicate the message of the passage in a single sentence so that it aids comprehension and lodges in memory
Sounds like a commentary	Sounds like a proverb
As long as necessary for accuracy and thoroughness	Fifteen words or fewer
Third person	First or second person
Past tense	Present tense
Example from Psalm 32: The psalmist praised God for the forgiveness he received after confessing his sin, because blessing attends the one whose sins are covered by God, but woes attend the one who tries to cover his own sin.	Example from Psalm 32: Cover or be covered.

I believe that every sermon should have a big idea for two reasons. The first relates to sound hermeneutics. Conservative exegetes believe in authorial intention—that the biblical authors intended to convey ideas to their readers. In any thought unit such as a paragraph in an epistle or a scene in a narrative, the author wanted to get a point across. To be sure, texts have many ideas, but our job in exegesis is to discern how those ideas relate to each other. They swirl around a central point. Texts are not a random hodgepodge. Stating the exegetical idea helps us articulate authorial intention. My second reason relates to communication. Sermons are most effective when they are laser focused. When the preacher cuts extraneous fat, listeners comprehend clearly. Reducing the essence of the sermon to one idea will increase its impact.

As you outline the text's flow of ideas, you can expect to see the following patterns of thought, common to human experience:

- problem-solution

- cause-effect

- contrast (not this, but this)

- chronology (first this happened, then this, then this)

- promise-fulfillment

- lesser to greater

- argument-proof

- explanation-application

- principle-example/amplification

Other patterns undoubtedly exist, and once you train your mind to think in logical categories like these, discerning flow of thought becomes second nature. Some of the patterns above use inductive reasoning, and some use deductive reasoning. Induction starts with particulars and moves toward a conclusion or principle. The first six patterns are inductive. Deduction starts with the conclusion or axiom and then explains, proves, or applies that idea. The last three patterns are deductive.

Here is an exegetical outline for James 4:13–17, with commentary on the flow of thought in italics:

1. Some of James's readers boasted about tomorrow (v. 13).

   Effect: The passage begins inductively with an example of boasting. This is the effect of the cause James will identify later in the passage (arrogance). The author places a hypothetical speech in the mouths of the readers to show them what arrogance sounds like.

II. James rebukes such boasting (v. 14).

Contrast: In contrast to the wealth of knowledge implied in the boastful opening speech, the readers actually know little. They do not know the future. They are as fragile as mist. The logical flow from verse 13 to verse 14 is contrast: not this, but this.

III. James contrasts boastful speech with submissive speech (v. 15).

Contrast continued: The author continues with the logic of contrast by creating another hypothetical speech. This second speech shows proper words that are submissive and humble, in contrast with the opening speech.

IV. The readers boast because they are arrogant (v. 16a).

Cause: The author has described and illustrated the effect (boasting), and now he reveals the cause: arrogance. Westerners normally think in terms of cause-effect, but the reverse, effect-cause, is also possible.

V. Boasting is evil, and anyone who knows this, but persists in boasting, sins (vv. 16b–17).

Summary: James pulls the camera back to present the broad landscape. He ends by summarizing the previous exhortation about boasting. (Another possibility is that he provides further argumentation why the readers should not boast.)

Here is an exegetical outline for Psalm 32:

I. Blessed is the one whom the Lord has forgiven (vv. 1–2).

Announcement of theme: David summarizes the whole psalm with this headline.

II. When the author tried to cover his own sins, the Lord disciplined him (vv. 3–4).

*Problem: David describes the trouble his silence brought—
the Lord's heavy hand of discipline. Tradition says that this
psalm grew out of David's personal experience—his sins of
adultery and murder, and his attempt to cover his own sins.
After the announcement of the theme, he describes how miserable he was when he refused to confess.*

III. Then the author confessed, and God forgave (v. 5).

*Solution: After experiencing the discipline of God, David
finally confessed and experienced the blessings described in
verses 1–2. The logical (and somewhat chronological) flow moves from
trouble to grace, problem to solution.*

> ### Clear structure of the sermon depends on crystal clear understanding of the flow of thought in the passage.

IV.   The author urges others to follow his example and experience God's deliverance (vv. 6–11).

*Exhortation: David exhorts the readers to learn from his experience. The
wicked experience sorrow, but the love
of God surrounds the ones who trust
him. Therefore, confess!*

Clear structure of the sermon depends on crystal clear understanding of the flow of thought in the passage. Do not rush this foundational step in your exegesis.

Second stroke: rephrase (and possibly reorder) the points as a homiletical outline

Using John Stott's metaphor of "standing between two worlds," the exegetical outline resides in the world of the text, and the homiletical outline resides in the world of the listener. Compare:

Exegetical outline	Homiletical outline
Past tense	Present tense
Third person	First or second person
Summarizes the author's thought	Summarizes your thought *from* the text *for* the congregation
Follows the textual order exactly	Usually follows the textual order, but can also follow "thought order"

I'll illustrate the last item in this chart in a moment, but first let me illustrate the top three items. In the examples that follow, notice that the outline no longer sounds like a commentary ("James told his readers to do such and such"; "David did this or that"). Rather, it sounds like a living soul addressing living souls.

Here is a homiletical outline from James 4:13–17:

I. Sometimes we boast about tomorrow (v. 13).

II. We should not do this, because our knowledge is limited and our days are short (v. 14).

III. Big idea: Rather than boasting, we should speak with humility and submission to God's will (v. 15).

IV. The cause of our boasting is arrogance (v. 16a).

V. Now that you know this, if you continue to boast, you sin (vv. 16b–17).

Here is a homiletical outline from Psalm 32:

I. Big idea (summary): Blessed is the one whom the Lord has forgiven (vv. 1–2).

II. Problem: When we refuse to confess our sins, we bake in the oven of discipline (vv. 3–4).

III. Solution: Confess your sins, and God will forgive (v. 5).

IV. Exhortation: Listen to God's wisdom and experience God's deliverance (vv. 6–11).

To return to the issue above—the issue of textual order and thought order—consider this helpful example from Donald Sunukjian (summarized from *Invitation to Biblical Preaching*, 56–64):

> Textual order: "Don't get mad when the paperboy throws your paper in the bushes." The arrangement is *response* (don't get mad) to *cause* (the paperboy throws your paper in the bushes).
>
> Thought order: A sermon from this "text" could rearrange the textual order into the more natural thought order of *cause-response*. This would help the listeners follow the sequence of ideas. Thus:
>
> I. Cause: Sometimes the paperboy throws your paper in the bushes.
>
> II. Response: When that happens, don't get mad.

Although expository preachers usually adhere to textual order, rearranging the points of the expository outline can sometimes help us stand between two worlds. Rearrangement can help us clarify the meaning of the text.

Here are two examples from the texts above. First is a homiletical outline from James 4:13–17, rearranged for inductive thought order:

I. Our knowledge is limited, and our days are short (v. 14).
   Transition: Yet . . .

II. In our arrogance we boast (vv. 13, 16a).

Transition: Therefore ...

III. Such boasting is sin (vv. 16b–17).

Transition: In contrast ...

IV. Big idea: We should speak with humility and submission to God's will (v. 15).

The flow of thought in the outline above moves inductively. Starting with the assertion that we are fragile creatures, limited and ephemeral, the sermon's final point is the big idea. The sermon has driven toward the big idea.

Another homiletical outline could be arranged deductively, stating the big idea first. For example, here is a homiletical outline from James 4:13–17 rearranged for deductive thought order:

I. Big idea: We should speak with humility and submission to God's will (v. 15).

Transition: Why? Because ...

II. Our knowledge is limited, and our days are short (v. 14).

Transition: Yet ...

III. In our arrogance we boast (vv. 13, 16a).

Transition: Therefore ...

IV. Such boasting is sin (vv. 16b–17).

Here is a homiletical outline for Psalm 32 rearranged for deductive thought order:

I. Big idea (solution): Confess your sins (v. 5).

Transition: As a result ...

II. Result: Experience God's deliverance (vv. 1–2).
Transition: In contrast . . .

III. Problem: When we refuse to confess our sins, we bake in the oven of discipline (vv. 3–4).
Transition: Therefore . . .

IV. Exhortation: Listen to God's wisdom, and experience God's deliverance (vv. 6–11).

The example above states the big idea early in the sermon and then returns to it in the last point. The next example, a homiletical outline of Psalm 32 rearranged for inductive thought order, saves the big idea until the last point:

I. Problem: When we refuse to confess our sins, we bake in the oven of discipline (vv. 3–4).
Transition: In contrast, what we truly desire is . . .

II. Contrast: When we allow God to cover our sins, we know peace (vv. 1–2).
Transition: Therefore . . .

III. Big idea (solution): Confess your sins (v. 5).
Transition: As a result . . .

IV. Exhortation: Listen to God's wisdom, and experience God's deliverance (vv. 6–11).

The examples above demonstrate that expository preachers have latitude when it comes to structure. Our normal procedure, once again, is to follow the exegetical outline when creating the homiletical outline, but pastoral wisdom will sometimes suggest that we rearrange the points into a different order.

Third stroke: develop the points

Now that you have summarized the text's flow of thought and have rephrased (and possibly reordered) the points, put flesh on the bones. Develop the ideas by addressing the questions the listeners will ask. (See Haddon Robinson, *Biblical Preaching*, 2nd ed., 75–96.) If they ask:

Listeners' question	Preacher's response
What does that mean?	You must explain. The preacher takes the stance of a teacher.
Is that true?	You must defend/prove. The preacher takes the stance of an apologist.
So what?	You must apply. The preacher takes the stance of an equipper or exhorter, urging behavioral response.

This stage of structuring a clear and effective sermon demands audience analysis. You have to know the listeners' level of knowledge, belief, and submission to the text. Listen to the points of your outline through the ears of your listeners.

Furthermore, these three developmental questions are psychologically sequential. That is, people will often believe what has been clearly explained to them, and they will often do what they believe. Conversely, they are unlikely to believe what they do not understand; and they will not act upon what they do not believe. I have discovered that many people will respond to the gospel in faith and repentance if we simply explain it clearly. But if we cloud their understanding, they will neither believe nor respond. Our Lord says in this regard: "When anyone hears the word of the kingdom and *does not understand it*, the evil one comes and snatches away what has been sown in his heart" (Matt. 13:19, esv, italics added).

Understanding—when well established, often leads to . . .
Agreeing—when well established, often leads to . . .
Responding

We fulfill all three functions—explaining, proving, and applying—by taking the truth to every seat, with Story, Example, Analogy, and Testimony (SEAT). Remembering that the human mind is a picture gallery, not just a debating chamber, we stand between the words of the text and the hearts of the people by communicating frequently at the bottom of the ladder of abstraction, using concrete support material. This means that you take a general truth, such as "God values justice," or a vague exhortation, such as "be good," and bring that truth down to terra firma, the world of your listeners. (See Figure 1.1.)

To explain 1 Thessalonians 4:3 ("Avoid sexual immorality"), we could state an abstract definition of the Greek term *porneia* ("a broad term that includes most forms of sexual promiscuity"), but we will also cite examples from current events, movies, or TV shows. When explaining, we move from the known to the unknown.

Take another example from 1 Thessalonians 4:8 ("Whoever disregards this teaching disregards God" [paraphrase]). Your audience analysis might reveal that the congregation disagrees. They feel that their sexuality has nothing to do with their relationship to God. They love God, and they are sleeping around. So to convince them that God really means what he says in verse 8, you might use an analogy of a play rehearsal. The director instructs an actor to move downstage, but the actor moves upstage. Time after time as the players run the scene, the actor

14

Abstract

Be good.

Be generous.

Give money.

Tithe.

Next week we will take a
special offering for the Joneses.

Figure 1.1. Ladder of Abstraction

keeps moving upstage. This leads to a rift between the actor and director because deliberately disregarding the director's instructions is a way of disregarding the director.

Other forms of support material also exist besides SEAT, such as quotations and statistics, but those forms work best when coupled with concrete forms such as SEAT. The human mind craves concrete images.

Type of support

Stories

Strengths and weaknesses

These are excellent at explaining, proving, and applying, but a single story can take three or more minutes. That time usually is well invested, but most sermons can afford only a few stories.

Example from James 4:13–17 (Our days are short)

Last year about this time, Deacon Smith was meeting with his small group on a Wednesday night. The phone rang, and the voice on the other end of the receiver stammered in choked and broken words: "Your son has been in an accident." (Finish the story.) We hardly need the reminder, yet the reminder comes to us in verse 15: We are as thin and as fragile as mist. Our days are short.

Examples

Strengths and weaknesses

These are brief instances, miniature stories. They can be as short as a few words. Our sermons should bristle with examples. They are efficient, interesting, and relevant. They are a prime way to adapt the truth to your particular group of listeners, helping you stand between two worlds. The only weakness with examples is that, being specific, they may not connect with some members of the audience. This can be overcome by using multiple examples. Somehow the human mind takes particulars and translates them into universals and then reparticularizes for personal identification.

Examples from James 4:13–17 (Our days are short)

- Daniel Boone made his own cherry wood coffin years before he died. He kept it under his bed, and when visitors came, he would pull it out and lie in it to show them how well it fit. This is how he reminded himself and others that our days are short.

- Trappist monks always have an open grave on the grounds of their property. When one of their number dies, they put him in that grave and then dig another.

In this way, they constantly remind themselves that our days are short.

- The smallest microbe, the most unlikely mechanical failure, or the least expected natural disaster is enough to convince us of the truth of verse 15—that our days are short. Our lives are a vapor.

Analogies

Strengths and weaknesses

Because effective communicators move from the known to the unknown, analogies help clarify new concepts. That is, an analogy turns on the hall light so that listeners will not stumble through a difficult verse. Analogy takes listeners by the hand and guides them through the maze. Analogies work best when followed immediately by real or realistic examples. A drawback is that they can be hard to create. You have to have the skill and patience of a poet to ask: what is this *like*?

Examples from James 4:13–17 (Our days are short)

- Job said, "My life is but a breath" (7:7).

- Moses said we are like grass that springs up and then withers (Ps. 90).

- Paul said we are like a flapping tent being dismantled by the wind (2 Cor. 5).

- David said that his days were "a mere handbreadth" (Ps. 39:4–5).

Note: to learn from three geniuses of analogy, read C. H. Spurgeon, C. S. Lewis, and G. K. Chesterton.

Testimony

Strengths and weaknesses

People long to hear how other people respond to the truth, especially how they are applying it or what keeps them from applying it. In particular, when done with humility and prudence, our listeners long to hear how the *preacher* is living the text.

Using John Stott's model once again, the bridge between two worlds is the preacher. God has ordained that truth be incarnated, so we are not backward about revealing our own questions and reactions to the text. Just make sure that your self-disclosure illumines the truth and the beauty of God. Don't turn the pulpit into the confessor's chamber or psychiatrist's couch.

Example from James 4:13–17 (Our days are short)

Last year about this time, as I was meeting with my small group on a Wednesday night, the phone rang. My brother informed me that . . . (Finish the self-disclosure.) I thought of the words of James 4: "What is your life? You are a mist." Our days are short.

Fourth stroke: link the points with clear transitions

Oral discourse occurs in time. It starts at, say, 11:20 and ends at 11:49. It is a fluid river of words that, once spoken, pass on never to return. The words linger only until the echo fades. In contrast, written discourse occurs in space. You are reading these words. You hold spatial objects—sheets of paper or an electronic device. With written discourse, the rate of communication is under the control of the receiver. You can read one sentence twice, ponder it, underline it, discuss it with the person next to you, skip it, or lay the words aside and return to them next week. You control the flow of information.

Not so in oral communication. The flow is under the control of the sender, not the receiver. Communication breakdown occurs frequently in oral communication because speakers forget that simple distinction. Those speakers state key concepts only once, as if they were writing, not speaking. They believe that once is sufficient, but in reality those key concepts are quickly engulfed in the current of words sweeping past the listener. Experienced speakers know that repetition and restatement are essential to avoid communication breakdown.

When we apply that axiom to the topic of this article—structure—we see that transitions are some of the key concepts that must be stated and restated. They help listeners stay up with our flow of thought. A good transition will feel labored and redundant to the speaker, but listeners will be grateful that you briefly freeze the river with deliberate redundancy, giving them time to catch up with the river of words. Most listeners have only a foggy sense of what we are talking about as we preach. Blessed is the man or woman who links points with clear, direct, fulsome transitions.

For example, imagine that you are done talking about the first point in your sermon from Psalm 32. You are twelve minutes into your sermon and are now ready to move into the second point. Being an experienced preacher, you know that the minds of your listeners have wandered in the past twelve minutes, so they need to be recollected. Unlike readers, who can review what they have read and who have visual markers like paragraph indentations and headlines, the listeners have only your words and your delivery to help them move from one idea to the next. Knowing that if you state your transition only once, the listeners will not differentiate that sentence from the other sentences flowing across their ears in the river of words, you need to more deliberately freeze the river momentarily:

I. Problem: When we refuse to confess our sins, we bake in the oven of discipline (vv. 3–4).

Transition: We have seen the problem: namely, when we refuse to confess, we experience the discipline of God. Now let's look at the solution, the way out of this dilemma. Rather than stubbornly refusing to confess, we come clean. We confess, we admit the truth about ourselves. When we mess up, we 'fess up. That is the solution to our problem. Verse 5 shows us that we should confess.

II. Solution: Confess your sins (vv. 5, 1–2).

Notice some of the features of this transition: it *reviews* the previous point, *previews* the coming point, uses synonyms to effect *purposeful redundancy*, and states bluntly the *logical relationship* of the points (problem-solution). To reiterate, such pedestrian transitions feel labored to the speaker, but listeners will rise up and call you blessed.

Fifth stroke: write the introduction and conclusion

The purposes of the introduction are well known: gain attention, surface need, and introduce the subject of the sermon or the entire big idea. The preacher desires involuntary attention, so that listeners are riveted to the Word. The best way to achieve that is with a crisp opening statement that quickly "promises" that the sermon will address needs. Surface need, and you will have all the attention you desire.

The purposes of the conclusion are to summarize and drive home the big idea. These goals are often accomplished with techniques like a simple review, an epitomizing illustration, or a well-conceived prayer. However it is done, the conclusion wraps a ribbon around the entire message to demonstrate its unity and move the listeners toward a specific response. I find that most pastors do well with their introductions but are hit-or-miss with conclusions. This occurs because we run out of time and energy in preparation, or we ourselves do not fully understand the unity of the message and its implications for everyday life. While application should be made throughout the sermon, the conclusion should bring the application to a burning focus.

Expository preaching involves labor and sweat, especially the wearying work of structure, but five sure strokes of the hammer on anvil can help us shape our sermons with clarity and relevance.

Jeffrey Arthurs is the professor of preaching and communication, and the chair of the division of practical theology, at Gordon-Conwell Theological Seminary. He is author of *Preaching with Variety* (Kregel).

HOW PRAYER TRANSFORMS PREP

*Ongoing prayer has an irreplaceable,
revolutionary role in sermon preparation.*

Michael Lawrence

If you're a preacher, I know you pray for your sermon at least once a week. As you're walking toward the front on Sunday morning, your prayers are flying thick and fast, and all with the same theme: *Help!* I don't mean you're in a panic. But there's no denying the vulnerability of that moment, when you feel your own inadequacy in the face of the awesome task of becoming the voice of God to your congregation. You know people are there who need to hear something more than an inspiring thought or a tip on life. They need to hear from God, and if it's going to happen, it's going to happen through you. But who are you? As Jesus said, "Apart from me you can do nothing" (John 15:5). That includes preaching, and so we pray!

But beyond that existential moment of truth each week, does prayer play a role in your sermon preparation? Should it? Beyond asking God to give you an understanding of your text and a heart for your people, is there anything more to do in prayer? I think there is. Too many of us preachers treat prayer as if it's simply a step in the process, somewhere between reading the text for the first time and finding our illustrations. What we need is to regain a theological vision of prayer in which it becomes the posture of the preacher, for before our people can hear from God through us, we must hear from God first. And hearing from God through his Word is the fundamental work of prayer.

Humility

Prayer is often described as the pouring out of the heart to God, and that is surely right. Even a brief glance through the Psalms demonstrates that. But in our postmodern age, that idea is all too easily misunderstood, even by the preacher. We live in a culture and time that values self-expression above all else. We don't want to sell out. We're suspicious of anything that comes across as artificial or produced. *Authentic, fresh, real* are our buzzwords. And it's affected the way we think about prayer; it's affected the way we pray. When we pray, we're keeping it real with God; we're telling him what's on our mind, what's going on in our heart, what we're concerned about, or what we need. And that's about it.

And that's a problem, because in Scripture, pouring out our hearts to God is never the point of prayer. It's only the beginning. The point of prayer, the end of it, isn't self-expression; it's realignment, as our hearts assume a posture of dependence and humility before God. How does prayer do this? It does it by placing our needs in the perspective of his sufficiency, by placing our problems in the perspective of his sovereignty, and by placing our desires in the perspective of his will. When we pray, we're not engaging in a monologue. Ours may be the only voice we hear, but we're definitely not the only ones speaking. Rather, in prayer, we're inviting God to have the last word with us, and for his Word rather than ours to shape and define us. As the psalmist declares,

> I meditate on your precepts
> and consider your ways.
> I delight in your decrees;
> I will not neglect your Word. (Ps. 119:15–16)

So not only the first step, but the constant attitude of the preacher in sermon preparation must be prayer. This means far more than a quick prayer for wisdom and insight into the text before we move on to the work of exegesis. Prayerful meditation on the text should be our posture throughout the week. For me, that means meditation and prayer on the text every morning as part of my own devotions. I'm not trying to get a jump on sermon preparation. Exegesis and outlining doesn't begin in earnest until Thursday. Rather, in prayer I'm seeking to humble myself before God's Word, allowing it to plow up the soil of my own heart, so that when I finally come to preach, it's not my agenda and my desires that control, but God's. Prayer humbles the preacher, so that he is a fit instrument in the hands of the Redeemer.

Instruction

What are the tools you use to understand the meaning and significance of the text you're going to preach on Sunday morning? Commentaries, software programs, and a good concordance immediately come to mind, but so should prayer. Through prayer, the author of the Scriptures, the Holy Spirit, gives the preacher spiritual insight and understanding. Again, as the psalmist says, "I have more insight than all my teachers, for I meditate on your statutes" (Ps. 119:99). One of the ways the Holy Spirit does this is through the illumination of our minds. Sometimes this illumination is given immediately (Luke 12:11–12). But I'm not really talking about mystical feelings or audible voices. Normally, this insight comes as we pursue the hard work of study—translation, exegesis, reading, and so on—but pursue it prayerfully.

The author of Psalm 119 doesn't claim to have no need of teachers. Ezra didn't just wake up one day understanding God's Word ("Ezra had devoted himself to the study and observance of the Law of the LORD, and to teaching its decrees and laws in Israel" [Ezra 7:10]). Even Jesus gave himself to study ("After three days they found him in the temple courts, sitting among the teachers, listening to them and asking them questions. Everyone who heard him was amazed at his understanding and his answers" [Luke 2:46–47]). But throughout the Scriptures, God's messengers seek to understand God's Word with the assistance and instruction of the Spirit in prayer.

Do you first pray the Scriptures before you try to preach them? One of the habits I learned from an older preaching mentor was to praise God in prayer for something I saw revealed about him in the passage I was going to preach—and not just privately. In our elders' meetings and staff meetings, we begin by reading the passage for the coming week and praising God for what we see about him in that passage. Week after week, I come away instructed about both the text and the God of the text. I will have thought that I had seen all there was to see in the passage, but as I pray with my fellow staff and elders, the Holy Spirit instructs me *through them,* and I walk away with a richer vision of the passage to be preached. As preachers, we may be the most theologically trained people at the prayer meeting, but the Holy Spirit is no respecter of diplomas. Through prayer, privately and corporately, the Spirit teaches the preacher what *he* has said, and what *we* need to say.

Sympathy

Preparing sermons is more than just figuring out what the text means. It's also about what the congregation needs to hear. And if you're like most preachers, you probably have an opinion about what your congregation needs to hear most. But all too often, that means our sermons are shaped as much by our own hobby horses as they are by the text or the Spirit. Whether the issue is abortion or feeding the hungry, world missions or personal evangelism, healthy marriages or community service, most of us have our favorite points of application. And even if you're not sure what your favorite issue is, your congregation probably knows what it is.

Through prayer, and specifically as we pray through our text for our congregation, the Holy Spirit moves us from what *we* want for *our* people to what *he* has for *his* people. The psalmist prays,

> Let me understand the teaching of your precepts;
>   then I will meditate on your wonders.
> My soul is weary with sorrow;
>   strengthen me according to your word. (Ps. 119:27–28)

In our congregations there are people who need a bigger view of God, who need to find hope in the midst of discouragement, and comfort in the midst of sorrow. In our congregations, there are people who need to know the power of God to forgive, restore, and reconcile through Christ. They don't need our agenda, our priorities, or our programs. What they need is the wisdom of God for their lives, *according to his Word*. As we pray the Scriptures for them during our sermon preparation, the Holy Spirit moves us to understand our congregation from his divine perspective.

In my own practice, this involves praying each day for some of my members by name out of the text I'm going to preach on. As I do this, I move beyond the circumstances of life—health, jobs, and relationships—to the spiritual realities that really matter. I feel their spiritual weakness and rejoice in their spiritual growth. I bear their burdens and sorrows and long for their future glory.

> *What happens when prayer moves from being an afterthought in sermon preparation to our every thought?*

Prayer like this produces divinely directed sympathy for the congregation, and that leads to divinely directed agendas in our sermons. We're not content any longer with applications that are little more than pious platitudes or personal hot buttons. Instead, through prayer, our sermon applications reflect the heart of God for his people, as he speaks to them through his Word.

What happens when prayer moves from being an afterthought in sermon preparation to our every thought? God will humble our hearts, illumine our minds, and enlarge our spiritual affections. Our people need to hear from God. It's his Word that saves them, his Word that conforms them to the image of his

Son, his Word that leads them through this life. How will they hear, unless we preach? How can we preach, unless we have first heard through prayer?

Michael Lawrence is pastor of Hinson Baptist Church in Portland, Oregon, and author of *Biblical Theology in the Life of the Church* (Crossway).

THE SPIRITUAL IMPORTANCE OF BEING AN EMOTIONALLY HEALTHY PREACHER

Key issues to address as we look beneath the surface.

Peter Scazzero

All preachers know that we need to prepare our souls to preach, but what exactly needs to enter into that preparation? Obviously it is not enough simply to punch the clock in prayer for a certain period of time, so what should we pray about? How do we discern the condition of our own souls? In this insightful interview with Peter Scazzero, author of Emotionally Healthy Spirituality, *we learn specifics about essential places to which we can turn our attention as we prepare our hearts to proclaim God's Word.*

You've written two books on what you call *emotionally healthy spirituality*. Could you provide a brief overview of what you mean by that term and why it's important?

Basically, it's a paradigm for how ordinary Christians can experience real transformation in Christ. It's taking people beyond outward changes and moving into the depths of their interior life in order to be transformed.

We look at this process in two broad strokes. First, we say that every Christian should have a contemplative life. Simply put, that means that each follower of Christ needs to cultivate a deep relationship with Christ—without living off other people's spiritual lives. That requires slowing down and structuring your whole life in such a way that Christ really becomes your Center.

Second, emotionally healthy spirituality means that emotional maturity and spiritual maturity go hand in hand. It's simply not possible to become spiritually mature while you remain emotionally immature. And emotional maturity really boils down to one thing—love. So if you're critical, defensive, touchy, unapproachable, insecure—telltale signs of emotional immaturity—you can't be spiritually mature. It doesn't matter how "anointed" you are or how much Bible knowledge you have. Love is the mark of maturity. Emotionally healthy spirituality unpacks what that looks like.

Why is there such a glaring need for this approach to our life in Christ?

I think it addresses some missing components in the way we approach discipleship, especially in the West. We can be very intellectually driven. We can also be driven by success and big numbers, so the idea of living contemplatively—sitting at the feet of Jesus like Mary in Luke 10—feels very countercultural to many of us. It's counter to our church culture as well, especially if you're a pastor. That's why this has such a huge impact on preaching: it starts with the transformation of the person in the pulpit.

So how does emotionally healthy spirituality change a pastor's approach to preaching?

That's probably best summed up by the thirteenth-century theologian Thomas Aquinas, who said that all of our preaching or teaching should be the fruit of contemplation. In other words, as a preacher I don't just study and exegete a text; I don't just find good stories to illustrate the text; I also let it pass through my life in such a significant way that the Word has transformed *me*—not just on the surface but in the depths of my heart. I am a different person because I've been steeping in this text all week long. I've sat at the feet of Jesus. That's the fruit of contemplation.

To me, that's the foundational issue for preachers. In my travels throughout North America, I think the great problem with preaching today is that most pastors don't take the biblical text and sit with Jesus. So we're preaching great sermons—clever, interesting, funny sermons—but I'm not sure those sermons are changing people's lives on a deep level.

So how do we see real transformation in people's lives through our preaching?

Again, it begins with the preacher. To change people's lives deeply through the Word, the preacher's life has to be transformed by the Word. At this point in my ministry, I rarely preach on a text that I haven't been meditating on all week long—and the goal is to allow God to transform *me*, not just write a good sermon. So before I get up to preach, the text needs to have changed me first.

For instance, I went for a four-mile walk today, and the whole time I was meditating and praying about my preaching text—the story from Mark about blind Bartimaeus. At times I was struggling with the text, wrestling with how it intersects with my life. By the time I get in the pulpit, I've often memorized the passage. Of course I still do my Greek and my Hebrew word studies, but as I enter my twenty-sixth year of preaching, I spend a lot more time praying the Word before God. I spend more time asking and listening to him about how he wants me to approach the text.

In your books you say that our lives are often like an iceberg; there's a lot underneath the surface, but it's largely hidden from us. How does that apply to what you're saying about our preparation for preaching?

As preachers the problem is that we usually don't take the time to look beneath the surface of our lives, at the rest of the iceberg, the 90 percent that people can't see. I know that I can easily ignore the immaturity and worldliness in my heart. As a result, I can diminish my preaching text because I'm stunted in my own relationship with Jesus. But when we wrestle with a biblical text, when we let it explore the hidden parts of our lives—that's when real transformation starts to happen.

For example, a couple of weeks ago I preached on John 21, where Jesus tells Peter, "I tell you the truth, when you were younger, you dressed yourself and went where you wanted; but when you are old you will stretch out your hands, and someone else will dress you and lead you where you do not want to go." Before I preached that verse, I had to let it sink into my own life. As I prayed about that verse, listening to the voice of Jesus to me through that verse, I realized how often I make plans without consulting him. God started peeling off the layers of my false self: Pete, are you really looking for happiness in security, control, and power, like Peter? Like him, are you just trying to do your own thing and go your own way?

I had to wrestle with the fact that a big chunk of my ministry has been focused on my will. In the end, God brought me to a new place of surrender to him and to his will.

Every week I need to listen to the Lord like that. The Word needs to pass deep into my life—underneath the surface. And that will bear fruit in my preaching. I can't get that from a book. You can't read that in a commentary.

Do you think part of our emotional-spiritual immaturity comes from getting too wrapped up in the preacher's role— that our identity is tied too closely to our sermonic success?

Absolutely. Number one, I need to be preaching to myself first. So every week I need to remind myself that I stand before God based on the righteousness of Christ alone, not on whether I preached a good sermon. So if someone says, "That sermon stunk," or, "That sermon didn't hit the mark for me," I don't need to get depressed or defensive. I can just say, "Okay, tell me why it didn't hit the mark for you." I don't expect to hit a home run every week. I offer God the best I have, and I let it go.

> *If I'm too concerned about what people think of me and how the sermon is going to come off, I don't think I'm ready to preach.*

One of the best things I have to offer people is what God is doing in my life through this text. I look for a clear outline with solid points and good illustrations, but they're not my highest priority. My highest priority is to be centered in the love of Christ. If I'm too concerned about what people think of me and how the sermon is going to come off, I don't think I'm ready to preach that sermon.

Since you started focusing more on transformational preaching, what other changes have you seen in your sermon preparation?

I definitely spend a lot more time thinking and praying through the sermon application. What difference will this make in people's lives? What does this passage say to the single mom, the stressed-out executive, or the questioning teenager? When people walk out the door, what are they going to do with this text?

Often I see two extremes in sermon application. There's the ultrapractical, how-to, four-steps-to-a-happy-marriage type of sermon that's almost all application. Those sermons are often theologically and historically empty. But then there's also the exegetically correct sermon that has almost no application. These preachers haven't allowed the text to pass through their own lives.

I'm preaching on blind Bartimaeus. We have six blind people in our congregation. How does this passage apply to their lives? My point can't just be that Jesus heals the blind, so come and get healed right now. I need to wrestle with this text and apply it to the lives of real people. That's hard work—whether your church is rural, suburban, or urban. It takes time. Honestly, I'm not sure how I'm going to apply this text, but I know I need to apply it to myself first. At this point in my sermon prep, I can sure relate to the people in the crowd who kept telling Bartimaeus to shut up. I also want to be more like Bartimaeus—desperately crying out to Jesus even when everyone around me is telling me to be quiet. Those are definitely points to explore as I seek to apply this text.

In one of your recent blog posts you wrote, "Unknowingly, some pastors use their flock as extensions of their own needs and ambitions." How do you think pastors can "use their flock" when it comes to preaching?

I've often heard preachers say things like "I have a fire in my bones, and I *have* to preach." But if you look underneath the surface of their lives, they're preaching has a lot to do with their own issues and needs. They are thinking about how they're performing: "What do people think of me? Did people like my sermon today?" If that is the case, the whole process of preaching focuses on us, not God and his people.

It happens in subtle ways, too. A while ago I had to pull aside one of the guys in our preaching team and say, "I have to tell you that you crossed a line in your sermon last week. At one point you were really funny, and you had people rolling, but it seemed like you started working the crowd on a level that wasn't appropriate." It wasn't a terrible issue, but it definitely felt egotistical or show-offy—and it detracted from the flow of the sermon.

As I look back on my own preaching, I wish I would have had someone to pull me aside and help me look underneath the surface of my life as a preacher. I learned so many things the hard way. Now I constantly tell younger preachers, "If you want to be a great preacher, learn Greek and Hebrew, learn a lot about church history; but first and foremost, learn to be with Jesus, develop a deep prayer life, and learn to love people." I've heard some brilliant sermons, but it didn't take a rocket scientist to see that the sermon was more focused on the person in the pulpit.

But how do you preach powerful sermons when you know you haven't arrived yet, when you know your life is still raw or immature? Let's say you're preaching on forgiveness, and you're struggling to forgive someone as you prepare the sermon. How should you approach that as a preacher?

That's the real beauty of preaching! Those are the most powerful sermons—when we know we're still in the process of growing in Christ. That's when God can really show up. You're going to preach the truth—the truth about Scripture and the truth about your life. Obviously, you're not going to say, "I'm struggling to forgive Joe Jones in the fourth row because he sent me a nasty letter this week." But during my sermon prep, I'm going to feel the hurts of life—pastors take a lot of hits—and I'm going to feel how impossible it is to forgive anyone. I can't do it in my own strength. Left to myself, I don't love my enemies.

That's why brokenness before God is so crucial in our preaching. Obviously, I hope I have some spiritual maturity, but on the other hand there are probably people in my church who are further ahead of me on the path of forgiveness—or many other issues. I'm not up in the pulpit saying I have this all figured out. In my preaching I'm always communicating: I'm a fellow traveler just like all of you. God has been teaching me some things through this text, and I'm struggling with this truth just as you are. I stand by the grace of God just as you do. You better not put me on a pedestal because I'm not worthy of being on a pedestal. If you put me on a pedestal, you'll be disappointed.

But you can still speak God's Word with authority. You can preach on forgiving your enemies, because it's true. "Jesus told us to forgive those who trespass against us because we're going to get hurt every day. So choose to do good to those who hurt you, even when you don't feel like it." But I can also say, "Friends, this is impossible. I know because I've tried. Only God can help you do it. It will take a miracle—but God wants to give us the miracle of forgiveness."

So preaching from brokenness and weakness isn't just a technique or a preaching strategy. It has to flow genuinely from your life.

I've been a Christian for thirty-six years, but I'm still such a beginner. We're always beginners. The cross is starting to make more sense to me these days—that the Christian life is all about being crucified with Jesus so that he might live through me. I love the apostle Paul's view in 2 Corinthians 10–13. Paul was clear that he was not a superapostle. He had a thorn in the flesh, but he delighted in his weaknesses. That's a very countercultural and even un-American approach to preaching.

There are some great speakers in the church today. I'm in awe of the gifts that some people have. But I feel like one of my contributions to the preaching conversation is this idea of preaching from our brokenness and weakness—that God's power flows through that. If God has given you great eloquence, then use that gift; but don't ever let that gift cloud where true power comes from. Ultimately it's the rawness of your life and your encounter with God's grace that becomes one of your greatest preaching gifts.

Actually, gifted preachers are the most in danger. They can get by, and people love it, but it's also possible that nothing significant is taking place. You can draw a crowd of people, but in terms of spiritual transformation, nothing is happening.

Here's the key principle behind preaching that leads to transformation in Christ: You can't bring people on a journey that you haven't taken. You can tell them about the journey, but they could read that in a book. But if you go on a journey with Jesus that has real depth, it will come out in your preaching. If you've been sidetracked from that journey with Christ—building a big church, or gaining people's approval, or being so busy you can't even think straight—I would say that God is telling you to slow down so that you can be with Jesus. Your people need you to spend time in prayer. Your people need you to be with God, so you can bring a real word from God.

Peter Scazzero is the founder and senior pastor of New Life Fellowship Church in Queens, New York, and author of *Emotionally Healthy Spirituality* (Thomas Nelson).

SIMPLY PROFOUND

Reality is complex. Here's how to write sermons that are clear and simple without being simplistic.

Duane Litfin

Most everyone who preaches knows what it's like to work hard and long on a sermon and then when preaching the message realize that in a sense we worked "too hard." In other words, the outline or the ideas are too complex or difficult for listeners to grasp. In this interview, Duane Litfin discusses how to find the clear simplicity that is the fruit of deep thinking.

What is simplicity?

Simplicity is certainly related to clarity. The more complex the message is, the more likely it won't be clear. But there's something about simplicity that has to do with the cleanness of the message, the cleanness, the unclutteredness, of the ideas.

Oliver Wendell Holmes purportedly said, "I would not give a fig for the simplicity this side of complexity, but I would give my life for the simplicity on the other side of complexity." In this quotation you have two simplicities. The simplicity on this side of complexity is oversimplification. It's simple, but it gets at simplicity the cheap way, by refusing to take into consideration all the complexity of the subject. And so it winds up simpleminded.

I don't like that kind of simplicity. Maybe it's the academic in me, but I thrive on nuance, clarity, genuinely doing justice to the complexity of the subject. I'm looking for the simplicity on the other side of complexity. Such simplicity takes complexity into consideration and strikes to the essence of it. Such simplicity makes sense of that complexity rather than avoiding it. That's the simplicity worth having. That kind of simplicity is profound and powerful.

> *The kind of simplicity we're after is not one that ignores complexity, but rather makes sense of it in a simple way.*

There's a danger, then, in setting complexity and simplicity in conflict, because the kind of simplicity we're after is not one that ignores complexity, but rather makes sense of it in a simple way. So a good sermon is simple in the sense that it is tied together around a central truth that makes sense of complexity. A good sermon will often be complex, but it will hang together. All that complexity will make sense, and the audience can assimilate it, because the complexity is given unity by a core something in that message.

When we lack that core, then we have all the pieces, but we don't have anything that makes sense of them or gives them coherence. That kind of complexity is hard on an audience. They're struggling to find that unity, trying to make sense of the complexity. They're trying to find what this part has to do with that part, and we're not helping them with it.

This is the genius behind the notion of developing a central idea in your message. I've taught for years with Haddon Robinson, who is often tied to so-called big-idea preaching. This approach says your message should be about one strong, large, significant, generative idea. Your message unfolds that.

In the case of expository preaching, that means you choose a passage that is a unit of discourse. The unit is a unit precisely because it has a central emphasis that gives it its "unit-ness," its unity. That's where you get your central idea. You don't force that on to the text. Good expository preaching develops the central idea that helps the audience grapple with the complexity inherent in virtually any significant passage of Scripture. So you haven't left the complexity of the text behind, but you have a simplicity to the message because you're on the other side of that complexity, helping the audience make sense of it.

What is the difference between the topic of a sermon and the main idea of the sermon, and what difference does this make in the simplicity of the message?

It's important to deal with the full idea of a passage, not just the topic. "Prayer" is not an idea; it's a topic. "Prayer is the source of our spiritual power"—that's an idea. You're predicating something about prayer. In a full idea such as this, you have a subject, which answers the question, what am I talking about? And you have a predicate, or complement, which answers the question, what am I saying about what I'm talking about? It's not till you have the combination of at least those two things that you really have an idea. If all you have is a subject, then your sermon will almost certainly be a pile of sticks. You're saying a bunch of different things about that subject that don't necessarily tie together around a central affirmation. That's a prescription for a kind of complexity that is hard on audiences. They're trying to play pick-up-sticks with the preacher's points and make some overall sense of them, but they're having to do it on their own.

Understanding the main idea of a passage requires clear thinking. If we haven't thought our way through clearly to that central idea, then how can we expect the audience to have clarity about what we're saying?

For that to happen, you have to think through the flow of ideas in that text, so that you understand why this sentence leads to that sentence, and to that sentence, from beginning to end.

Absolutely. This is the mark of good exegesis. You're thinking with the author and trying to understand. The author speaks in ideas, not topics. The passage doesn't have one topic after another; instead, it has one idea after another. The passage has sentences, paragraphs, units, and you're trying to think through them with the author. It's out of that—what the author is saying—that you get your message.

In fact, in your preaching outline you need to use ideas— fully stated subject-complement ideas—not just for the central idea of the message, but for every point in your outline. Write a detailed outline of your message. It's a great discipline to make every point in your outline a full, grammatically complete sentence. There should not be one place where you have just a topic word or phrase. This forces you to be clear in your own thinking, which will help you to be clear for your audience.

This discipline enables you to look at your outline and ask the question, how do these subpoints develop this superior point? You are much better able to see whether they really do.

This is helpful because unfortunately we can arrange an outline in good outline form, but if we look at the Roman-numeral idea and then the *A, B,* and *C* ideas under it, we find that the *A, B,* and *C* ideas aren't coordinate to each other, and they really don't support the Roman-numeral idea. But the outline formatting fools us; it makes it look like they do. Well, there's a breakdown here in the clarity of the preacher's thinking, and that's going to come across and lead to a complexity that will hurt our audience's comprehension.

I've seen expository sermons that include every idea in a long passage. Such messages strike me as having a density of ideas that people in our culture, who don't have a great attention span, will have trouble following.

If we're working as we should, we do a lot of exegetical homework in the text. As a result we can feel an obligation to dump that whole load on the audience. In the time frame you have, that often works against your audience's ability to understand. If you had more time to develop this passage with your audience, to the point where you could unpack every idea and show how it relates to the whole, your audience might be able to handle this. But often you don't have time. You have to pick and choose wisely.

This brings us back to the importance of the passage's central idea and its development. Give people as much of that central idea and its development as possible, all the way through to its relevance for us. Why does God want us to know this? What difference does he expect these ideas to make in our lives? You should dip down into the minutia only as far as you can go and still achieve that. The point is for people to hear a word from heaven. Here is what God is saying in this passage. Here is the difference he expects this to make in our lives.

When I pastored a church in Tennessee, one thing I did to address the problem of having too much to say in one Sunday morning sermon was to unify the two Sunday messages. We had a morning and evening service. The Sunday night message would come out of the overflow of the Sunday morning message. In virtually every scriptural passage, there are rabbit trails, tangential issues, or things people have questions about. Of course, if you don't have a Sunday night service, you can do this in a midweek Bible study or small group meeting. I often had people tell me they appreciated the unity of the day instead of having two series going on at the same time. And it sure helped my prep time.

How do we recognize before it's too late that our message is overly complex?

If you do a detailed, full-sentence outline, you will likely know immediately. You'll look at what you have and realize, I'll never get this all in. If you have twelve major points, that's way too much for people to take in through the ear. Perhaps some listeners could take that in through the eye if they had time to read it. But when they have to take it in for the first time through their ears, and you only have so much time, you have to limit the number of major points.

A good rule of thumb is three. A three-point sermon is not just a cliché; there are some substantial, conceptual reasons why having three main ideas makes a lot of sense. At any rate, if I'm past five main points, I know I have a problem.

I think of major points in a message as being movements, like acts in a play or movements in a symphonic piece. I call them movements instead of points and think of messages more organically than mechanically. Some outlines just clunk along

46

mechanically. I think of the outline more like a map. Here's where I want to wind up, and here's where we're starting. From there we'll go to here, and from there we'll go over here, and so on. I'm taking people with me on a journey almost like on a map.

What part do illustrations play in achieving simplicity and clarity?

An effective communicator moves up and down the ladder of abstraction. Abstract ideas are fleshed out by concrete illustrations, and the concrete is explained and made sense of in the light of larger ideas. So we need the interplay between the concrete and the abstract.

The idea of sticking with one or the other doesn't make sense. If we stick with the abstract, we're a long way from where people live their lives. But keeping everything at the concrete level doesn't make sense either. Postmoderns often look down on propositional abstractions, but that's crazy. The genius of the human mind is the ability to abstract. Dogs can't think of justice. Mosquitoes can't think of differential equations. In fact, the most brilliant human minds are the ones that can do the highest level abstractions.

What you don't want to do is stay up at the abstract level; nor do you want to settle at the concrete level. You need the concrete to flesh out the abstract, and the abstract to explain the concrete. You keep moving up and down.

That's what Einstein did, wasn't it? He explained E = MC² with pictures.

Einstein's thought pictures were first for this own thinking. He found them helpful in conceptualizing what he was after. But they were also helpful in explaining his ideas to others. He used the image of a train whistle's changing sound as it passes us to explain the red shift of light. This is what every effective communicator does. When we move up and down the ladder, it enables us to be profound and yet simple.

So there again, going back to what we said earlier, it probably is not a good idea to set complexity and simplicity against each other, as if the one sacrifices the other. Reality of whatever sort tends to be complex. The best kind of simplicity is thus the kind that helps us make sense of that complexity, not overlook it.

Who is a helpful example of dealing with complex ideas in a simple way?

It's a cliché, but that's the genius of C. S. Lewis. In his essays, found for example in *God in the Dock* or *Mere Christianity*, he's dealing with sophisticated ideas, but he manages to put them simply. Lewis is about the only author I go back and reread on a regular basis for this very reason. He just captures things. He's dealing with profound issues, but he makes them available to us in wonderfully illuminating and simple ways.

Duane Litfin is a writer and speaker. He served as president of Wheaton College in Wheaton, Illinois, and is author of *Public Speaking* (Baker).

IF YOU DISLIKE SERMON PREP

*Writing a sermon always requires hard work,
but there are ways to work smart and take
unnecessary hardship out of preparation.*

Bill Hybels

*When someone is as well known a preacher as Bill Hybels, we
naturally assume there is nothing he would rather do than write
sermons. Not so, says Hybels. In this interview, we find what he
has learned about how to optimize his sermon study, even though
he would often prefer to minister in other ways.*

**I recall hearing you say at one of Willow Creek's preaching
conferences that sermon preparation is not your favorite
thing to do.**

That's true. When I and others assess my spiritual gift mix,
my top spiritual gift is leadership, second is evangelism, third is
teaching. I believe your top gift can flow quite naturally out of
your heart. Your second gift may be a bit more difficult to express. When it gets down to your third gift, that will be a little
tougher to express. It might feel more like work than play, and

certainly that's where my teaching gift fits in. I've had a love-hate relationship with teaching since I stepped up to teach for the first time almost forty years ago. Sometimes I think heaven will be no new sermon preps. I'll be a happy guy.

Is disliking message preparation a fault?

I have tried not to develop a complaining spirit about message prep. Teaching is a gift God has entrusted to me, and I need to be a servant before God and steward this gift carefully and joyfully. If teaching is more difficult for us, we have to "up" the structure and discipline. We need to get ahead of the game by developing a pattern of preparation that mitigates the difficulty. We can't say, "It's difficult," and collapse under the weight of that reality. The exact opposite is true. We need extra measures to make sure there is room in our schedules and there are resources around us, so we can do it well.

What are your disciplines?

First, I have to find the most creative part of my day, which is early morning. I have to take the best part of my day to put the best energies I have to the preaching task, because it is so difficult for me. So I create space in my daily life to stay ahead of the prep game.

If I fall behind during a week, I'm tough to live with come Friday, because it preoccupies me. Whereas if I'm following my pattern, which is to work about three hours each morning of the week, and if I feel as though I'm making the right progress, then when I'm done with my daily sermon prep time, I can begin the meetings I have and leave the sermon prep in God's hands. I can flip over into the use of the gift that is most enjoyable for me, which is leadership, and give myself joyfully to that for the rest of the day. I know that at an early hour to-morrow morning I can't use leadership gifts; now it's teaching prep—here we go.

I do this Monday through Friday, and then on Saturday morning for three hours I do the final polishing. We have a Saturday evening service, so I'm up teaching on Saturday night.

For those who dislike sermon prep, can there be a problem beneath the problem?

If you create the space and time for God to work in your preparation, yet week after week you feel that God isn't moving, the page is empty, then my advice shifts into another gear. My next questions are: What are you reading? How much are you reading? Rich thoughts don't come out of thin air. Rich thoughts come from reading. You have to read more than you teach to keep your cup full.

Next I would ask, do you feel too alone in the process? If your answer is yes, my response is, it's only as lonely as you want it to be. If I'm heading into a new series and feel too alone, I'll gather two or three trusted people and say, "I'll buy you lunch, but this is for brainstorming. I'll pop for the food, if you'll come with ideas." Sometimes the fog lifts when I engage the minds and hearts of others.

If none of this helps a person, then I go into personal stuff. What else is going on in your mind? What concerns are pressing in that crowd out the creative process? Is there marriage tension? Do you have a wayward child? Are you worried? Do you have a dying parent? What are the other issues in your life? Let's deal with those. Let's see if we can alleviate them a bit Let's give them over to God, so that when sermon prep comes, your spirit is freed up.

When your systems are in place, do you ever like message preparation?

Most people who have preaching as their top gift actually like the entire process. They like the reading, the creative part. They enjoy building the outline, collecting the illustrations. They absolutely love the actual delivery of the message, being up there with God's Word in their hand. When they're done, they feel fulfilled and can't wait for Monday morning to roll around to start the process again.

Now, if the gift is lower in your gift mix, then all those parts of the preaching process have a diminished thrill factor. Each part will require more discipline and won't give sheer recreational joy. In my case, when I'm delivering a message, I'm thinking, "Oh, good, it won't be long, and this will be over." When the message is done, I'm thinking, "Thank God, that's over, and I can do other things for a while." Even if I sense that God is really using the message, I get much more enjoyment from using my leadership or evangelism gifts.

So not everyone should expect to like message preparation. What should they expect?

If the gift of teaching is anywhere in the top three of your gift mix, if you supply the discipline and carve out the time when God can work, if you are reading, you should anticipate that the Spirit of God will meet you in those carved-out moments. You should expect to feel the activity of God in your mind. Over the course of that week of sermon prep, you should expect to notice times when God is at work and doing his part in this supernatural process.

You should expect holy-ground moments. There have been times when I have written a few paragraphs, stopped, gotten down on my knees, and prayed, "God, thank you for another holy-ground moment. These thoughts are higher than my thoughts. These are insights into the Scripture I don't have on my own. The greatest miracle with this sermon already happened. When I deliver this message, some people will think I had more to do with it than I really did, so I want to stop and acknowledge before heaven that you did this, and you get the glory. So thank you, God, that you gave me this gift, I get to use it, and I can feel your hand in it."

This is what keeps me going.

What else do you do to overcome the challenges of writing a sermon?

Pastors need to figure out the appropriate number of new sermons for them to give each year. Out of fifty-two Sundays, many pastors who have preaching as their number-one gift will select a number beginning with four, say forty-two or forty-five. Anything less than that, and they would not feel fully engaged or used. Those of us with preaching in rank two or three or four in our gift mix would probably have a number in the twenties or thirties, because it would debilitate us to preach forty-five times a year.

Every senior pastor has to do that self-analysis and then have a leadership talk with the elders or board and say, "Can we set an expectation that is congruent with where preaching is in my gift mix and the time I have to create great new sermons?" Some boards will say, "Look, we pay you to do this. We want forty-eight sermons." Sometimes that means the church gets twenty good sermons and twenty-eight bad ones. They're overrevving the pastor's engine, and everybody pays.

At Willow Creek when I came to clarity on this, probably fifteen years into the church, the elders and I agreed that creating new sermons twenty-five to thirty times a year is the absolute max that is healthy for me. So we introduced team teaching. It wasn't a well-known concept in the U.S. church. My limitations demanded that we get other teachers involved, and of course we looked for teachers who had teaching as their number-one-ranked gift. One of the great joys of my life is to be part of a teaching team instead of shouldering that complete burden myself.

I also get candid feedback on my messages from trusted advisers in the congregation. I've done this for at least twenty-five years, and it helps me feel as though I'm not in this thing alone.

Getting feedback is very sensitive, of course. I recommend that you ask three to five people, would you be willing to give me constructive, emotionally and spiritually intelligent feedback when I preach? Be sure to tell me all the good things, because after I've preached I'm emotionally exposed.

I ask people to do the evaluation in an e-mail and to wait until Sunday evening. I don't need it five minutes after I get out of the pulpit, because usually I'm just looking for a place to hide. By Sunday evening I get a half dozen e-mails from the people I've asked to do this, and they'll take the talk apart a bit and commend the parts they felt God used. This is very helpful to me. It gives me accountability.

You're also known for taking a summer study break.

Teachers need a finish line. You don't want to get up on Monday morning and say, "This is how Monday mornings are going to feel every week for the rest of my life"—facing a blank sheet of paper and six days away from a brand new talk. I think some teachers get so overwhelmed by that feeling they just decide they can't take sermon preparation that seriously, that it's overwhelming. So they lower the standard of their preaching.

So my approach has been to schedule a finish line. I can get fired up on Monday morning if I can say, "Okay, here we go— only eleven weeks. I've got eleven more brand new sermons to do, but then comes my break, when I can refill my bucket. I'll be able to read eight or ten new books and get ahead of the sermon prep game. I can cool my jets. I can rest my 'on switch.'"

Every communicator knows how you manage energy. If you have to give a talk on Sunday morning, you don't flip your "on switch" just five minutes before you get up to preach. The switch goes on either Saturday night or Sunday morning: "Wait a minute, I'm preaching, I have to get my head in the game. I have to get in the zone." Well, if you have a finish line and a break to your preaching cycle, you can turn that switch off for a while, let your emotions cool, and rebuild a sense of hunger.

> *Every teacher I know is better for letting the gun barrel cool off a bit, reloading, and then coming back in a better frame of mind.*

Because we have a teaching team at Willow, I might preach three or four weeks in a row, and then others teach for one or two weeks. That's a mini finish line. But then in July and August I don't do much preaching. In addition to using the teaching team, we bring in guests. So during the summer I take at least a four-week period when I'm not putting new talks together, so I can fill my mind and heart again.

If you take two weeks off or four weeks off, whatever the appropriate time is, and you refill your bucket, then you come back to the pulpit and you're glad to be there. You have a fresh anointing, fresh wind, fresh fire, fresh ideas, fresh material.

Every teacher I know is better for letting the gun barrel cool off a bit, reloading, and then coming back in a better frame of mind.

Bill Hybels is pastor of Willow Creek Community Church in South Barrington, Illinois, and creator of the Global Leadership Summit. He is author of *The Power of a Whisper* (Zondervan).

CONFESSIONS OF A
MANUSCRIPT PREACHER

I'm a better preacher when I semiread a sermon.

Mark Mitchell

I have a recurring nightmare. Having grown up in the Roman Catholic tradition, I'm kneeling in the dim light of the confessional booth. "Forgive me, father, for I have sinned."

The deep voice on the other side of the thin wall responds, "What sins do you wish to confess, my child?"

I'm startled. I know that voice. It's not the voice of my priest, but the daunting voice of my homiletics professor! I think to myself, "I wonder if he knows." Feeling exposed, I go on and confess my sin: "Doctor, please forgive me. It's true. I do it. I do it every Sunday. I . . . I . . . I . . . preach from a manuscript!"

Okay, that's far-fetched, but you get the point. Manuscript preaching isn't just marginalized, it's ridiculed. In most homiletics courses, preaching from a manuscript is considered a historic relic that's as useful today as an eight-track tape. If it's talked about at all, it's mentioned on a list of things never to do.

Experts give various reasons for dismissing the use of a manuscript. Most guilt inducing is the claim that using a manuscript blocks us from being led by the Spirit of God. I once had a classmate share with me in dramatic testimony fashion that he'd vowed to God never to use a manuscript again! In his mind, to do so would be depending on himself rather than the Holy Spirit. His assumption seemed to be that for the Spirit to work he needed to be free from the straitjacket of prior thought.

Another reason for dismissing manuscript preaching has to do with delivery. People say that those who preach with a manuscript seem disconnected from the congregation. Their cadence is less natural. Being tethered to a manuscript prevents their own personality from shining forth. Their words seem to come less from the heart and more from the script. Who wants to come to church and listen to a lecture that has as much vigor as a high school civics class?

There is truth in both of these claims. If we are a slave to our manuscript, we certainly could be less sensitive to the Spirit's promptings in the pulpit. And if we use a manuscript poorly, reading word for word, we certainly will seem disconnected from the congregation. But neither of these things are necessary in using a manuscript, and so, like Linus and his blanket, I still bring one with me to the pulpit.

I've learned I'm not alone. Effective preachers past and present have used manuscripts. What worked in Jonathan Edwards's day won't always work today, but manuscripts have long been used by inspired African American preachers as well as many of today's most effective preachers. Recently I have been worshiping at other churches—large churches with well-respected pastors—while on sabbatical. In each case, the pastor skillfully employed a manuscript while preaching. These preachers believe the Spirit of God anoints not just their preaching but their preparation; not just what happens in the pulpit but also in the study, the results of which are a well-crafted manuscript.

The advantages of manuscript preaching
I've found many advantages to preaching from a manuscript

First, writing a manuscript can ensure we say things well. A well-reasoned argument and precisely crafted words and sentences are an asset in the pulpit. Duane Litfin states, "It is quite startling to see how often writing a manuscript can reveal problems with the speech. . . . Weaknesses in our grasp of the passage, or soft spots in our presentation of it, make themselves known. Without the step of preparing a manuscript we perhaps would not discover these problems until too late."

Of course, writing a manuscript doesn't mean we must use it in the pulpit, but having it in the pulpit can also ensure that we say things the way we wanted to say them. I'm much less likely to drift from my subject or add something that wasn't needed or I may later regret. Using a manuscript can also help me stay in my allotted time.

Second, having a manuscript allows me to relax in the pulpit. Because I'm not worried about remembering the next thing I'm supposed to say, more of my own personality can actually come out. Maybe this is because I'm an introvert. In his book *Introverts in the Church*, Adam McHugh argues that introverts prefer preaching from a manuscript because we have a slower mechanism for word retrieval in public speaking. (I think that means I don't think well on my feet.) When my tongue is searching for the right word or phrase, I often come up empty or fall back on clichés. Someone has said, "A good sermon remembers itself." That may be true when it comes to remembering an outline, but remembering a well-crafted phrase or a key transitional sentence coming out of an illustration is different. For these, the security of a manuscript quiets my nerves and frees me up.

This is especially true on those mornings when emotionally I'm not at my best. Recently I spent the night in the trauma unit of an emergency room with my eighteen-year-old son. He'd been in a serious car accident with several friends. Thankfully, they all came out of it with minor injuries, but it was an emotionally exhausting night. I got home at about 5:00 a.m. Sunday morning, and within two hours I was on my way to church to preach two sermons. Having a manuscript to preach from was a crutch without which I couldn't have stood on that difficult morning.

> The security of a manuscript quiets my nerves and actually frees me up.

Third, having a written manuscript makes it easier for your church to offer printed sermons for further personal study and use in small group Bible studies. At our church we upload my full sermons to our church Web site promptly, and each week we offer a printed sermon from the previous Sunday for those who want to take it home for further digestion or even to pass it on to friends. We have further edited some of these messages and used them as "position papers" that deal with issues and questions that are frequently asked by inquisitive disciples.

How to use a manuscript with skill

The key to using a manuscript is using it well

First, you must write for the ear. Your message isn't meant to be a literary achievement, but rather a personal word from God. Robert Jacks's book *Just Say the Word: Writing for the Ear* is a must for manuscript preachers. Academic lectures are full of *therefores, indeeds,* and *in conclusions,* but we rarely talk like that. When we write for the ear, we'll contract words: *don't* instead of *do not, can't* instead of *cannot,* and *wouldn't* instead of *would not.* We'll also avoid using *that* as a connector. Instead of saying, "Jesus said *that* he was the Way," we'll say, "Jesus said he was the Way."

These may sound like small things, and they may tweak some of what we learned in freshman grammar, but it will make a world of difference in keeping your listeners engaged. When I'm finished with my manuscript, I always say it aloud. I want to test how it sounds to the ear. When I say it, does it sound formal and stilted? Is this the way I would normally talk to people?

Second, don't read your manuscript word for word. This means you must know it well enough that you need only an occasional glance at the page and can still maintain eye contact with your listeners. Obviously this means reading and rereading your manuscript before preaching. Don't try to memorize it, but internalize the flow and train your eye to where the material is on the page so you don't struggle to find your place each time you look down. Most of the time, when I glance at the start of a paragraph, I know the essence of it, and I've nailed down the phraseology well enough that I don't have to read it word for word. It will also help a great deal if you arrange the material on the page in such a way that it's easy to pick up. Use a large font size, plenty of spacing, and bold-face type to help you pick up your key points. Some preachers use only the top half of the page to avoid having to look too far down (bobbing their head) and to keep their line of sight closer to the listener.

I've found I need to follow certain parts of the manuscript more closely, while others I hardly use at all. For example, when using a personal illustration, I try not to use my manuscript. I want to relive that story, and to do that I'll often move out from behind the pulpit and speak in a more direct and personal way. I also often do this at key points of application.

Third, when reading the Bible, read directly from the Bible, not your manuscript. I've seen manuscript preachers never even open their Bibles because the words of their text are printed in their manuscripts. Some don't have a Bible with them at all! But, for me, there's something about reading the text from a Bible in my hand. This also gives me another opportunity to move out from behind the pulpit and address people directly as I read from God's Word.

Fourth, don't let your handling of the manuscript be a distraction. Obviously, when using a manuscript, you have to turn the pages. That can be a distraction if you don't do it well. I've seen manuscript preachers, each time they turn a page, lick a finger, use awkward pauses midsentence, and make more noise than the crying baby in the back of the church. The bottom line is, you don't want the manuscript to be a distraction. So I use plastic covers over each page in a loose-leaf binder. This allows me to turn or slide each page quietly. Some manuscript preachers like to keep two pages of text in front of them, which of course minimizes the number of times you must turn the page. Perhaps most important is knowing your manuscript well enough that you can anticipate what's ahead and not pause or even look down while turning the page.

Finally, remain sensitive to the Spirit's prompting while using your manuscript. He directed you in the writing of your manuscript, and he can direct you in the preaching of it as well. There are times when he will nudge you to say something not in your manuscript. It may be an added insight into the text that doesn't occur to you until you're reading it publicly. It might be an image or story that comes to mind, or even another passage of Scripture that strengthens your point.

Manuscript preaching isn't for everyone, but neither is preaching without one. My hope is that you will use the method that fits your own personality and style, as well as that which serves your particular church the best. If you do that, by God's grace even your homiletics professor will be proud.

Mark Mitchell is pastor of Central Peninsula Church in Foster City, California.

A WEEK IN THE LIFE OF AN
EXTEMPORANEOUS PREACHER

*Preaching for the ear—orality—rather than for being
read—literateness—requires not less preparation,
but a much different method of preparation.*

Dave McClellan

*For years I've been studying the differences between oral and
literary approaches to sermon preparation and delivery. In fact, I
focused an entire dissertation on it. Even more formative for me
than the theoretical study, though, has been the chance to develop
an oral homiletic before the patient congregation that I serve. The
weekly practice has evolved into a rhythm that feels normal now,
even though it's miles from how I was originally taught to preach.
I've seen an oral approach yield dividends in terms of better rap-
port, freedom, and passion in preaching.*

*Our church now has a young intern named Ben who wants to
learn preaching, and it's been great fun to pull him into the process. The following is what I might say to him to summarize my
homiletical week—a literary account of an oral practice.*

Ben,

Considering that all our recent conversations on oral homiletics have been, well, oral, I thought perhaps it might help you if I put some things down on paper. You know how I feel about the value of face-to-face communication, but I also have to admit that the world of text does have some advantages. In terms of longevity and precision, writing still works well!

So maybe you could see this as a supplement to our conversations. I won't really go into the theology of orality and the historical grounding since we've previously covered all that. But it occurs to me that I've never really explained how to put this into practice as you prepare a message. After all, when you get to the point where you're preaching every week, you have to find a rhythm that you can sustain week in and week out. That's different from preaching just one good message or even preaching once a month. The weekly grind is demanding, and here's where an oral approach has some real advantages. It doesn't save time over a purely literary approach, but it can use nonstudy time more effectively (as when you're preparing while you're showering or driving or taking a walk).

This outline is not a rigid structure, but more like a generalized week in the life of an extemporaneous preacher. Not every phase happens on the same day every week. But there is a common sequence of preparation that has developed over years of working it out. So here goes. See if this helps.

Monday

You want to get a feel for the chapter. We've talked previously about why it's worth taking a whole chapter at a time, so I won't get into that now. You also know how important it is to preach all the way through a biblical book. Context is everything when it comes to hermeneutics, so there are great hermeneutical advantages to staying in a particular book.

So on Monday start by reading the chapter quietly to yourself, and then out loud as well. You have to get all your literate preparation done early in the week, so you can jump to oral composition and preparation way before Sunday. This is when you work in the original languages and try to hear the text with fresh ears. Pretend you've never heard this before. This is tough, because our familiarity with passages tends to push us to premature conclusions. Listen to the author's flow of thought. In other words, chapter 7 doesn't arise in a vacuum. It follows chapter 6. So you still have to be hearing 6 when you read and study 7.

After sitting with the text for a while, try to picture the flow of thought in chunks. There's a chunk on this, which leads to a chunk on that, and so on. If you can picture and describe the flow of thought from chunk to chunk, that's all you want out of Monday. Oh, this is when you can also record yourself reading the chapter into your laptop. Then dump it to your iPod and take it on the road to listen to while you drive or walk.

Tuesday

Finish any research in history, culture, geography, and so on. Here's where you get the great advantage of staying in a particular book. Once you're up to speed on the historical background to Romans, you can use that for sixteen weeks. That saves you the work of reading the history and culture every week (as you'd have to do if you bounced around to a different book each week). Of course the congregation benefits, too, by that consistency.

On Tuesdays you can begin the dialogical preparation. As you know firsthand, my weekly discussion group is open to any guy in the church who wants to participate. You saw how the dialogue not only invests the guys in the sermon, but how it also starts to uncover connections between the text and real life. The questions and observations that come up there add fuel to the homiletical fire, and some form of them often ends up in the sermon. This is sermon preparation happening in the oral instead of the literate environment. You have to adjust your thinking here, because you've always thought of sermon prep being a literate skill. This is more of an oral skill, but it counts. It's real sermon preparation the old-fashioned way.

Wednesday

Start talking the sermon as you drive around, not the whole sermon, just pieces of it. Refine your thinking by speaking. All the thoughts will end up being spoken on Sunday anyway, so why not begin now? Why foster an addiction to notes and outlines, only to try to wean yourself away from them? Better never to develop the dependence.

So as you speak about observations and the flow of thought, illustrations will come to mind, some out of dialogue with others, and some from your own life and experience. At this point, just keep them in your head. Don't even write them down. That's one thing you have to change as you start preparing this way. When you have a good idea (often while driving), you'll want to pull over and write it down so you don't forget. What you eventually realize is that your mind will never develop its innate oral capacities if you constantly revert to text. That's like trying to improve your mental math skills by using a calculator. Calculators don't build anything except dependence upon calculators.

But as you talk and ruminate about ideas from the text, certain ones tend to rise to the surface. These are usually the ones you think people will be able to catch, universal experiences that everyone can picture. Some of these stories you can sense are ripe for telling. Maybe it's a metaphor that connects the text to contemporary life, a historical story, or a current event. It's something that draws out the meaning of the text. It's a story you find yourself wanting to tell. This is oral composition.

Thursday

It's time to start organizing these ideas into a flow. This is important, because extemporaneous delivery is not impromptu or spontaneous (both of which connote a lack of preparation). In contrast, though extemporaneous delivery has some spontaneous overtones, it is, in fact, highly prepared. But it's prepared orally with narrative structure instead of being prepared literately with outline structure.

Traditionally, when preachers write an outline, they are trying to capture the essence of a text and then form those ideas into an outline with multiple points. Since the biblical author didn't have enumerated points, the preacher may end up contriving the points in the outline. In other words, the preacher may squeeze things out of a text to fit into an outline template. The resulting points are the preacher's valiant effort to pull meaning from one communicative environment into another.

You don't have to work that hard, because the flow of thought is already there. That's because the original author's brain was already working to connect to an audience when the text was first penned (or spoken, depending on the passage). Why should you try to improve on that? Your job is just to gather in, digest, and reanimate the chapter. So the chapter itself, and nothing else, will always be the basis for the sermon. Just take the author's chunks of thought and explain, illustrate, and apply them. That's it. It's that simple.

Here's where the road map concept comes in. Most chapters don't have more than three or four chunks. Then if you add an introduction and conclusion as additional chunks, you end up with five to seven chunks in a sermon. These are sort of like points, but different. When sermon points have a parallel structure, as so many sermons do, the sequence of points can usually be switched around without consequence. So if your sermon is "Five Ways That God Cares for Us," switching the order of points 4 and 5 probably doesn't matter.

Chunks are different. Since they are tied to the author's flow of thought, they have to stay in order, because an author is usually moving sequentially and logically (or maybe emotionally) from chunk to chunk. Another difference is that many preachers write points in just a phrase rather than in a full idea expressed in a complete sentence, while chunks are fully developed units of thought.

So when you build your road map, start with your introduction and devise a little icon or stick figure that will visually call it to mind. Then develop an icon for each chunk that captures the way you'll illustrate it. It might be a Band-Aid, tree, rope, snake, or cell phone. Next you just arrange your little icons into the right order and add your concluding icon. Put them on a winding path instead of a straight line so that you get the sense you're moving along a journey from chunk to chunk.

When you're done with your road map, you have a piece of paper with five to seven icons on it. No words. Not a single word. It's all visual reminders or oral preparation.

Friday and Saturday

Friday is my day off, so I don't do any formal preparation. Although with as much work as I've done, I can't help thinking about some of the illustrations. You can still be alert for new or better metaphors and connections to flesh out the chunks. Saturday works the same way. You don't actually have to do much on the sermon except maybe think about it as you drive. When you go to bed, you can just run through the flow of thought in your head. Or if you wake up early, do the same thing before you get out of bed. If you're doing mindless tasks like mowing or painting or shoveling snow, you can ruminate on things as you work.

Sunday

On Sunday you'll want to get up early enough to do the last part of your preparation. You can sit and whisper through the message from chunk to chunk, or you can go to the room where you'll preach and walk around in that setting and practice. Here's when you work on transitions between chunks and uncover any remaining foggy thinking. If something doesn't flow well, just back up and keep speaking it until it does. You'll find you don't usually need your paper road map now, since you can remember the five pictures in your head. That brings a sense of freedom. When you're well prepared, you can see the pictures and know where you're going at all times.

Finally, on Sunday morning you need to forget, in a sense, everything you've learned—not your road map, just the ways you've spoken it up till then. You want to discover these truths with the people, not report to them, so you have to back up to where they are. They don't "get" this chapter. So you have to start where they are and move them along chunk by chunk. Convince yourself, and you'll convince them. Argue yourself along, and they'll eavesdrop on the process.

Here's where extemporaneous preaching makes a difference. Although you know what you'll say, you don't know how you'll say it until you look at real faces. You have to talk to real people. You can't decide everything in advance, or your sermon will feel cut and pasted into the room. The people in the room have to decide how things are described, the exact word choice and sentence structure. If those people are helping you decide how to say things, they get the sense they're participating in it instead of just listening. They won't be able to put their finger on it, but they'll have the subtle sense that you're sharing a space instead of invading their space.

> *Although you know what you'll say, you don't know how you'll say it until you look at real faces.*

Of course that means sometimes you won't be precise. You might have verbal glitches, unfinished sentences, and redundancies (all of which are problems only in the world of literacy). You might even adapt on the fly and add something that wasn't on your road map. That's okay too, because whatever else you have, you'll have fluency. You'll have fluency because you started speaking these things on Tuesday and Wednesday instead of Saturday. That's the problem with literate preparation: it doesn't move to the oral environment until the last minute. You, on the other hand, have been talking about this message all week. So it literally is on the tip of your tongue.

I hope that helps you sense the flow. Try it the next time you preach and see how your own flow develops. Remember, the sermon is always already there in the text. But it's frozen there in print. Your job is to melt it back to life.

Dave McClellan is pastor of The Chapel at Tinkers Creek in Streetsboro, Ohio. He created the video series *Preach by Ear*.

HOW TEAMWORK
ENRICHES A SERMON

Our message needs to come from the Lord,
but God can speak to us through others.

Dave Stone

Years ago I wrote a book called *Refining Your Style*, for which I interviewed twelve top communicators. I asked each of the twelve if they ever had someone read their message before preaching it. Every one said yes except for one: Franklin Graham. I remember asking Franklin, "When you finish writing your sermon, do you send it around to other people to read it over to see if they have any suggestions on a better way to say something or a different route to go?" There was this long pause; then he said, "Why would I ask someone else to tell me what the Holy Spirit has laid on my heart to preach?" There was another long silence . . . and I went on to the next question.

Franklin Graham's take, and it's a valid one, is that if the Holy Spirit lays something on your heart, you should preach it. That approach is a good match for his personality and style of preaching. But he's more gifted than I am, and he's probably in better tune with the Holy Spirit's promptings. For me and my house, I need more sets of eyes on a sermon, or else I'll butcher a text, say something I'll regret, or miss out on something.

I have prepared messages in community since I came to Southeast Christian Church twenty-two years ago. The norm for me before Southeast was to write sermons on my own. I might have had someone read a manuscript, but I never had people looking creatively to suggest ideas or giving input at several stages in the process.

> *I need more sets of eyes on a sermon, or else I'll butcher a text, say something I'll regret, or miss out on something.*

I don't oppose preparing in isolation. There have been a few times when I wrote a sermon that God just laid on my heart. I sat down, and four hours later I got up, and it was 90 percent done. But for the past twenty-two years I can count on one hand the number of times that's occurred. I've found it's better to get more insight, to have folks looking over my material and shooting holes in it.

Constructive critiques

Years ago, even though Bob Russell and I worked on sermons together during the week, we decided to critique each other on Saturday nights after the first service. Bob was my hero, and the first few weeks that we did this I said things like: "I liked this point." "I loved the story you had at the start of the introduction." "That was a great quote." "Boy, that joke went over great!" I went through the whole sermon saying all these positive things, and at the end I'd say, "Don't change anything. It was awesome. You the man."

After two weeks of that, he said, "I appreciate the encouragement, but this really isn't helping me. You need to feel free to share your constructive ideas. That's the only way I'm going to improve."

So the next week we sat down after Bob's message, and with a straight face I looked at him and said, "What in the world are you doing in the ministry?"

Eventually we struck a happy medium of about 80 percent encouragement and 20 percent suggestions.

If you have multiple service times, sometimes the most helpful critique comes after the first message, because reading a sermon and hearing it preached can be two different things. Sometimes someone will say, "When I read that, I thought it was good, but when you delivered it, it was so much better than I expected." Or vice versa. Sometimes a sermon looks great on paper, but when you preach it in front of a crowd, it feels flat. You think, "Well, maybe it was just me," but then someone on the preaching team gives feedback that confirms it.

I like humor and used to use more of it than I do now. I remember Bob Russell saying things like, "I don't think you need that joke in the second part of your message." Then he would say, "But if you have it in there for your own sake, then keep it in." He was saying something that's essential to working on a sermon together: The person who is in the pulpit holds the keys to the manuscript. He has to preach what he feels comfortable with. Others can submit ideas, but the person who is preaching will probably take only two of every five suggestions, and that's because they are trying to let their personality come through. They're saying, "That might fit for you, but that's not my style. That would be a stretch. People would know that's not me."

Team prep can also be detrimental if you try to throw a bone to a staff person by using something of theirs that's not of good quality. You think it will be a nice pat on the back for that person, but you've got to think of the dozens, hundreds, or thousands of people who will hear the message. You want to give your congregation the cream.

How to help each other

Over my time at Southeast, working together on sermons has taken different forms. Initially it was primarily Bob Russell and I. Then for several years, six or seven pastors from different churches in the region came to Southeast on Thursdays to work on a sermon together. We would all prepare ahead of time. All the messages had the same topic, text, and title. We'd go around the table, and each person would share how they were going to approach the subject. That ran its course, and now I meet weekly with the preaching team from Southeast: our preaching intern, teaching minister Kyle Idleman, and another staff pastor who is a great preacher. We discuss the material of whoever is preaching that weekend.

In a way it's weird for me to write about preparing a sermon as part of a team, because I have an independent streak that bristles at that idea. I don't want you to think there's a team of six people who are writing my sermon, and all I do is look at it and say, "I like this, I like that, I don't like this," and then just preach it. That's not what it's like. Most of the time we bring 70 percent of our own stuff and then get a few ideas from one another, like how to improve an outline, how to conclude the message, finding a quote for the introduction. So it's an authentic process.

Here is how the process works right now. We have three meetings for each sermon. First, we have a creative planning team that meets about a month before the sermon to come up with ideas for graphics, props, or a special touch.

Second, the Monday before the sermon—we already have our titles and our texts in mind that have come out of that previous meeting—we have a meeting with our preaching department and our worship department. Ideas come, and they spur other ideas. It primes the pump.

Third, the preaching team comes back together on Thursday. When I'm the one preaching that Sunday, I send a manuscript to the other three guys, and they come to that meeting prepared to say what they like and what suggestions they have. I've written 80 percent of the message, but I'm getting a set of eyes to look over my shoulder and say, "Well, some people might hear it this way," or, "That phrase might seem inflammatory to some people." After that Thursday meeting, I spend Friday and Saturday making little adjustments, cutting out two pages and adding two pages, as I fine-tune the message.

Two of the guys from the preaching team hear me preach the message at the first service on Saturday, and they will leave me a voice mail and tell me ways they think I could improve the sermon for the next service.

The right people for the team

How do you put together a team of people to help you?

First, it's important to get input from the right people. If those helping you are not excellent writers or communicators, they're probably not helping the cause.

It takes time for a study group to gel, because at first your defenses are up. You come in with your baby; you've worked hard on this message all week. You can start to bristle when others say, "I don't think this point is valid," or when those who've listened to your message in the first service say, "I didn't feel that you did a good job telling that story. Either you need to know it better, or you need to cut it." If that person doesn't have your respect, you're going to dismiss the advice, be defensive, or stop listening to their counsel. As I said earlier, others need to offer 80 percent encouragement and 20 percent challenge.

Finally, if you're starting a team, I recommend trying it short term. If you start it on a trial basis, like for a six-week series, you can ask a group of people to help without then hurting their feelings if you don't continue to seek their advice. Say, "For the next six weeks, would you be willing to tell me what you like about my sermons, as well as what you don't like? I'll need you to lace it with a lot of encouragement, but I need your insights and perspective." If you start short term, you always have an exit strategy. If you find someone extremely helpful, you can ask that person to help you every week. If you don't disclose to each person who else is on the team, no one will have hurt feelings. Eventually you will stumble on to one or two people who can really help you.

Such people allow you to reach more segments of your congregation. For example, Mark Jones, one of the pastors who used to be in our Thursday preaching group, was a history buff. I'm weak in history. As we talked about our plans for our sermons, he would often share a story about the Civil War or an Old Testament story that had not occurred to me. Sometimes I would use that story in my sermon, and it was not unusual for people to say to me afterward, "I loved that story."

What Mark allowed me to do, because we were in a study group together, was to scratch an itch in the minds of my listeners that on my own I couldn't scratch. I naturally share a lot of sports, business, and travel stories, but when I can share something from history or science—two areas that I struggle with—that sermon steps up a notch. More people engage in what I'm saying because I've touched on their interests.

So, all in all, my experience with working with a team on my messages has been positive. Getting input from others can smooth the rough edges of a message, add strong tributaries to the sermon river, and broaden my perspective.

Dave Stone is pastor of Southeast Christian Church in Louisville, Kentucky, and author of *Refining Your Style* (Group).

FOUR WAYS TO GET OUT OF A "ONE PITCH" PREACHING RUT

Expanding your range can help your people grow.

Matt Woodley

Jimmy Jackson almost made it to baseball's big leagues. He sure had a good run with the Minnesota Twins' AAA farm team. Pitching coaches routinely clocked his fastball in the mid-nineties. Yep, you could always count on Jimmy's fastball.

Of course that was Jimmy's downfall too: he *only* threw fastballs. No curveballs, sliders, or change-ups—just blistering fastballs in roughly the same place: belt-high and smack down the middle. So after a while every batter knew what was coming. There's a good chance he could have made the Twins' starting lineup—if he could have had at least one more pitch. But for the rest of his short career, Jimmy just kept slinging that trademark fastball.

If you're a real Twins fan, you probably know that Jimmy never existed. I made up his story to offer an important insight about preaching: just as pro baseball players get stuck in pitching ruts, pastors can get stuck in preaching ruts. One-pitch pastors usually have one good pitch, but, as in Jimmy's case, that might also be their weakness. After a while the sermonic predictability gets old. Even worse, one-pitch preachers sometimes fail to preach what the apostle Paul called "the whole counsel of God." As a result, in some ways their hearers remain spiritually stuck and stagnant.

I should know because I often struggle with my own one-pitch preaching rut. Honestly, it's a good single pitch that I'll call pastoral preaching. During my sermon preparation, I'm almost always acutely aware that I'm preaching to broken people who need the tender care of the great Shepherd. (And I'm also acutely aware of my own need for grace.) I suppose the guiding verse for my sermon preparation could be Matthew 12:20:

> He will not break a bruised reed
>   or quench a smoldering wick
> until he brings justice to victory. (NRSV)

In my preaching, I don't like "breaking" people. I assume that they are pretty broken up by the time they walk into church. I want to apply the balm of the gospel to that brokenness. So Sunday after Sunday, I wind up and hurl my grace-pitch—fast, straight, right over the plate.

A preaching friend of mine who tends toward prophetic preaching once told me something that I needed to hear: "As preachers if we cease to confront people in our sermons, we abandon them to a lack of growth." I don't like to think that my preaching abandons people to a lack of growth, but my friend has a good point.

Of course there are other preaching ruts. The prophetic preaching path can also become a rut. We need bracing, in-your-face sermons from prophetic preachers, but after a string of Amos-like messages about all those "fat cows of Bashan," listeners start craving a spoonful of tenderness. Or there are one-pitch doctrinal preachers. These sermons drip with rich theological insights, but the application may be lacking. Some preachers use the one pitch of practical, how-to sermons—four steps to a better marriage, five ways to excel at work, or six principles for handling your finances. Some pastors get into illustration ruts. I know preachers who always, and I mean *always*, pepper their sermons with illustrations about their kids. On any given Sunday, I learn more about their kids than the Scriptures.

Preferring one preaching style isn't always a bad thing. God has wired every preacher with a unique combination of spiritual gifts and pastoral burdens. That's why our favorite preaching pitch feels authentic. It's our sweet spot, and everybody loves sweet spots. But it's even more than that. We keep using our favorite approach to preaching because it works. For instance, over and over again I've watched God change lives as people encounter his grace and mercy.

> *To help people grow, at some point preachers need to step out of their preaching sweet spot.*

On the other hand, to preach the whole counsel of God and help people grow as fully formed disciples of Jesus, at some point preachers need to step out of their preaching sweet spot. People need to see Jesus both as the tender Shepherd and the roaring Lion. Great doctrine by itself won't transform hearts. Practical principles—even biblical principles—could produce very busy but theologically ignorant church members.

So how do we preach outside of our sweet spot? More specifically, during our sermon preparation, how do we get ready to use a change-up when all we've ever thrown is a fastball?

Assess your own preaching style

Begin assessing your style by honestly reviewing your sermon history and your preaching tendencies. What is your favorite (or perhaps your only) approach to preaching? Do you tend to be primarily doctrinal, confrontational, an explainer, pastoral, how-to, inductive in structure, deductive in structure? Do you always use an opening story followed by three parallel points? Do you always preach from the New Testament epistles or some other biblical genre? Do you always develop your main points using original-language word studies? Is there any way that your sermons become utterly predictable? How would you describe your repertoire—or lack thereof—of sermons?

The best and quickest (but also the scariest) way to assess your preaching style is to get feedback from your listeners. Sometimes people will talk to you face to face. When they do, don't get defensive and quickly try to dismiss their negative comments. Even your crankiest critics may have valuable advice about your sermon tendencies. I once had a friendly but frustrated parishioner tell me, "I used to like all of your illustrations, but now I can count on your illustrating a sermon point with one of three sources: a story from your hometown, a sports analogy, or a quote from C. S. Lewis and his friends." I went back through my sermons, and he was right. My illustrations were a blur of Minnesota, football, and the Inklings.

Even your frustrated critics may have a point. If someone keeps telling me, "Your sermons aren't deep enough (or practical enough, or challenging enough, or biblical enough)," that may be about my critic's issues; then again, if I hear the same complaint enough, it could be a clue that I'm resorting to one-pitch preaching. What are critics really asking for?

If people don't give you direct and honest feedback, just ask them to tell you how they experience your preaching. For example, about midway through my nine-year pastorate on Long Island, I started asking a few key people (and not just my biggest fans) the following questions: How would you describe my preaching in one or two sentences? If you could summarize the main theme in my sermons, what would you say? What do you want more of in my preaching?

Long Island people are typical New Yorkers: they'll tell you what they think. So they told me to stop being so nice and just let them have it. They really meant it. Actually, in some ways they were exasperated by my one-pitch preaching rut. One guy told me, "Hey, look, you're not in Minnesota anymore. Whatever you have to say, whatever God lays on your heart, don't beat around the bush; just say it. We're dying for you to get in our face and challenge us more."

It takes a lot of humility to assess your preaching style. After all, we've usually spent hours crafting our messages. By the time we get done preaching, our messages feel like they're wrapped up with our self-worth. But as we find our true identity in Christ (not our preaching about Christ), we can slowly release our defensive attitudes and face our limited approach to preaching.

Ask different questions of the text

Most of us approach our sermon text with a largely subconscious set of questions. For instance, based on my temperament and spiritual gifts, during my sermon preparation I tend to focus on questions like these: How does this passage offer God's comfort to wounded people? Where's the grace and encouragement in this passage? How can I bring the healing touch of Christ to sin-sick people? Obviously, those are great questions, but they shouldn't be the *only* questions I ask during sermon prep.

At some point during my sermon preparation, I need to expand the standard questions I ask. For me that means asking questions like these: Where does this text confront our sinful tendencies? How is God calling his people to repent? Based on this passage, what idols do we need to confess and renounce? How is God stretching us to love and serve others, especially the poor and marginalized? Where does this passage call people to grow? Am I allowing the Spirit to lead me in this sermon, or am I just reverting to my preaching default because it's safe and easy? I suggest that you become a collector of questions. You can't and shouldn't use them all, but questions can lead you to thinking in ways you typically would not.

Most of those questions cut against the grain of my default sermon prep process, but if I don't intentionally expand my sermon prep questions, I will fall into a preaching rut.

Be willing to stretch your preaching comfort zone

I suggest that every once in a while you intentionally preach a sermon that breaks from your comfortable pattern. As a historical example, at one point the English revivalist John Wesley was preaching formal, traditional sermons within the church walls of established Church of England buildings. Meanwhile, Wesley's friend George Whitefield was watching God work in miraculous ways through his outdoor preaching services. The thought of preaching in the open fields repulsed Wesley. He thought it was highly improper. But in his journal dated March 15, 1739, Wesley noted the day when God added a curve ball to his preaching repertoire. "At four in the afternoon," Wesley wrote, "I submitted to be more vile, and proclaimed in the highways the glad tidings of salvation, speaking from a little eminence in a ground adjoining to the city, to about three thousand people." From that point on, Wesley's journal records that he routinely saw mass conversions through this "vile" approach to preaching—in the field.

I have a friend who needed to be "more vile" in his approach to preaching. For the most part, he prefers to preach theologically rich, three-point sermons that offer pastoral encouragement. That's his sweet spot as a preacher. But recently his senior pastor asked him to preach a sermon as part of a series on raising children in today's culture. Since my friend has adult children already, they asked him to preach on the topic of launching your teenagers into adulthood. He definitely struggled with the idea of preaching a five-step, how-to sermon on a practical issue. In some ways it felt like a colossal sellout.

But as he prepared for the sermon, he started to reconsider his assumptions by asking a few key questions: Does God's Word really have nothing to say about how to launch children into adulthood? Can't we search the Scriptures and find principles—solid, biblical principles—that relate to this pressing need in our culture? My friend went on to preach his five-step, how-to sermon, and many people found it enormously helpful. He probably won't preach that way every week, but he grew as a preacher by changing his approach to preaching for that one Sunday.

Learn from other preachers

This is perhaps the best argument for reading or listening to the sermons of other preachers, especially preachers who don't preach just like you. There are some fine and famous preachers who sure don't preach like me; in other words, they sound as cranky as Jeremiah, and I'd rather hear an encouraging message from Barnabas. But the body of Christ needs preachers who don't preach like me. And I need preachers who don't preach like me. How else will I learn to stretch my approach to preaching? By reading or listening to their sermons, essentially I'm saying, "Show me how to throw that curve ball. Show me how to be more prophetic (or practical or pastoral or doctrinal or gospel-centered) in my messages."

For instance, a friend of mine told me that he's been reading sermons by a preacher who had once been a lawyer. My friend has a gift for mercy, and it usually shines through in his sermons. But my friend has been learning another angle on preaching by reading these sermons. The preacher applies his rigorous, logical mind to his sermons. He uses a relentless lawyer-like approach to arrive at his "closing argument": will you accept Jesus or not? My friend knows he can't be like the lawyer-preacher, but he can sure learn from him. Sometimes he needs to bring a case and draw people to a certain conclusion based on the evidence of the text.

Author and preacher D. A. Carson was heard to quote approvingly this anonymous bit of wisdom for preachers about listening to others' sermons: "If you listen only to one preacher, you become a clone. You listen to two, and you become confused. You listen to fifty, and you are on the edge of being freed up to become wise and your own person."

Conclusion

Becoming a multipitch preacher doesn't happen overnight. And for many preachers it doesn't occur early in their preaching ministry. Most preachers have to grow into and then identify and enjoy the one approach to preaching that becomes their signature pitch. So although growing as a preacher involves some hard work and painful insight, in the end it's worth it. God's Word gets proclaimed with a richer power, and your people will experience new avenues for spiritual growth.

Matt Woodley pastored churches in Minnesota and on Long Island (most recently the Three Village Church) and now lives in Chicago and serves as the managing editor for PreachingToday. com. He is author of *The Gospel of Matthew: God with Us* (IVP).

HOW TO PLAN AND PACKAGE
A YEAR OF SERMON SERIES

The series "brand" can unify what a church says and does.

David Daniels

In this interview with David Daniels, pastor of Pantego Bible Church in Fort Worth, Texas, we discuss the unique opportunities and demands not only of writing a sermon series, but of aiming to tie together the sermon series of an entire year under one theme.

A sermon series demands more from the preacher in the way of "packaging" than a stand-alone sermon. You need to choose a series topic and title, and perhaps a series metaphor, subtitle, and text. You need to divide the topic into individual sermons and Scriptures that cover a certain amount of terrain each week. You title and perhaps subtitle each message in a unified way. You may write a marketing paragraph for the church Web site to stir interest in the series, and so you're thinking about how to connect with culture. What process do you follow?

I start planning for the next year around September. Typically I begin my thinking with what I perceive are the needs of the church and where I feel that God is leading us and me, whether it's a greater focus on mission, community, personal sanctification, or another topic.

Something we started this year and plan to do again next year is to give the whole year a theme. The year 2011 was the Year of Mission, so every sermon series related to what it means to be missional. Some of the series have been overtly about mission, like our March series called Pandemic: The Global Outbreak of the Gospel of God. Before Pandemic, we had a two-week series on orphan care. For the summer, I taught a twelve-week series on James; the central theme was, if we're going to be a church on a mission, then our best missional testimony is how we live. I also preached a series about practical evangelism called Kingdom Starter Kit, followed by a six-week series on the Holy Spirit's role in our mission.

So the year is a series of series.

Exactly. Before we get specific in planning the series for the year, though, we look at the calendar and block out the weeks where each series will fit. We build our preaching calendar around the nonnegotiables on the church calendar. In January I always preach a vision series. Easter and Mother's Day are set. We have to take into account the rhythm of people's church attendance when it comes to times like spring break at school.

We also factor in when new people enter the church versus when they are settled in the church. Naturally our series during the seeking times will be slightly different from that during the settling times. There have been times when I've scheduled a series that seemed great because it fit a five-week block in September, but then I realized it was a settling series when it should have been more of a seeking series. We should have scheduled it for November.

Once we know the blocks of time we have to work with, I schedule each sermon series and then begin to plan individual sermons in order in a series. I tend to move from week 1 being more theological to the final weeks leaning more practical, from the *why* to the *what*. By the time we get to the end of a series, we are leading people toward personal and corporate application of the spiritual truths they have learned.

Once I've determined the flow of the sermon series, I begin work on "branding," which means the words and images we will use to communicate the series. A recent series on the Holy Spirit we titled Third Person, and we chose titles and graphics that reflected the mystery of the Spirit. A series on the book of Jonah we titled Life Overboard, and a six-part series on the Bible was TXT MSG. We coordinate our titles, visual elements, staging, and collateral materials, not for the purpose of being slick, but to help people stay focused in one direction. Often we will see if there is a way to brand ministry initiatives during a series (homeless outreach, new class, and so on) in line with the series so that people can see how what we hear is connected with how we live.

One series that has become a recurring part of our annual calendar is what we call Rewind. It's been a tremendous success. On the four Sundays in November, I revisit the highlights and key principles of the several selected series from the year, one Sunday per series. We exclude our Easter series, the series leading up to November, and our vision series. This usually leaves about four series for the year.

Instead of a series being heard and forgotten, the Rewind series reignites and reminds the congregation concerning where we've been. Rewind says, this has been the life of our church for the past twelve months; let's not forget the significant principles God has taught us. Rewind also benefits the teaching team by giving some breathing space when we don't have to prepare new material before we hit the Christmas season.

How do you determine the needs of the congregation as you plan the series for the year?

As I think about series, I spend a lot of time listening to my fellow pastors in the church, sharing ideas from my heart and letting them reflect back. I really value my staff, because I know how much greater contact my staff has with our people and what's going on in their lives.

That's one reason I don't plan sermon series alone. I meet with our worship pastor, media director, executive pastor, and a couple of other creative people. Four or five times a year, we'll take a whole day and work on the next couple of series in broad brush strokes, talking about the overarching metaphors and ideas we want to communicate. Typically I bring to that meeting the ideas God has put on my heart, but that team helps to flesh out the ideas.

They're honest enough to say things to me like "I think if you preach it that way, you will deliver the theological goods, but I don't think that will change anybody's heart." We'll go back to the drawing board and work on it some more. We're always asking, "How is this truly going to change lives?"

In addition to giving honest feedback, creative teams are beneficial because they just keep you working ahead. When you work ahead, the series become more creative and good ideas eventually become great ones.

What mistakes should we avoid when putting a series together?

We can overbrand things. We can become enticed and titillated by our great titles, incredible posters, and clever wordsmithing and count on that to carry the day rather than on excellent study of Scripture and humble preaching.

I've also learned how easy it is to get lost in our metaphors. If we've decided to use a circus metaphor for a series, but then when I get into the sermon text for the week the apostle Paul is using a marathon metaphor, now I've got several metaphors to deal with. Metaphor on top of metaphor is impossible to communicate.

There is also a downside to working ahead. Because we prepare a Bible study guide for people to use a week prior to a sermon, I must choose a text, title, and topic ahead of time—before I have been able to give a deeper study of the text. More than once I have discovered that my title, metaphor, or focus wasn't exactly aligned with the text.

But hiccups like this don't overshadow the wider benefits of planning series far ahead. For instance, we try to take the other major initiatives going on in our church and cobrand them with the current sermon series. When we did the Pandemic series, we were raising money for a Bible translation. We shifted our initiative for a couple of weeks to fit with the series, and we put the Pandemic logo and graphics on our advertising to help people

> *We treat the branding that goes with a series as one more way to help people catch the vision of what we're trying to communicate.*

understand that this initiative fits where we are right now with the series, that what they're hearing on the platform makes sense with what's going on in the church. We try to connect ministry with the message.

What makes a series interesting enough to people inside and outside the church that they keep coming back and inviting others to join them?

At the end of the day, it's not clever branding; it's relevant preaching. If I'm not handling the Word of God with integrity and showing people how truth makes a difference in their lives, all my creativity would be nothing more than smoke and mirrors. In the end we hit the mark when we faithfully preach God's Word in a way that opens up the possibility for genuine life transformation.

We treat the branding that goes with a series as one more way to help people catch the vision of what we're trying to communicate.

David Daniels is pastor of Pantego Bible Church in Fort Worth, Texas, and cofounder and executive board member of Beta Upsilon Chi (Brothers Under Christ), a national Christian fraternity.

PSYCHED TO PREACH

Why I look forward to another Sunday with enthusiasm.

Lee Eclov

You've seen football players waiting in the locker room before a big game. Quiet. Intense. Stretched out on benches or the floor. Eyes closed. Earbuds channeling music. Then it's time. Coaches call them to arms, shoot them full of aural adrenaline, and out they come! They blast through the paper wall while their fans cheer and their teammates huff and fist pump.

Maybe I could preach better if we did that before the worship service. I could stretch out on the floor of my study with an iPod and get pumped on Keller or Chan or Tony Evans. Maybe I could huddle up with the elders behind the platform, hands stacked, voices starting low: "preach. Preach! PREACH!" And then with a controlled burn I stride to the holy desk. The congregation holds their breath.

Yogi Berra said of baseball, "Ninety-five percent of this game is half mental." Preaching is about the same. We learned how to exegete a text, how to structure an outline, and how to stand and deliver. But somewhere along the line we need to learn the mental game.

I know that it is my God-ordained responsibility to faithfully deliver his Word whether I'm jazzed or not. We preach by faith. We preach even on Sundays when our hearts are heavy or our minds are dull. The Spirit's anointing—his *unction*—does not always come with an adrenaline rush. But I can still get psyched. *Psych* is a transliteration of the Greek word *psuche*—soul. That works for me. Let's say I've got to get "souled" up before I preach. But it won't work to follow the example of athletes before a big game. Preachers have different motivations.

> I've got to get "souled" up before I preach.

Heavy lifting

Usually the first time I read my text, it seems one dimensional, like Flat Stanley, and as light as the paper it's printed on. As I study, pray, and think, it is almost as though, one word or phrase at a time, the print grows bold faced and bigger and even heavier, as though the very ink gains weight. Gradually it is as if the passage begins to inflate from its flat folds and take on a more lifelike shape. Jesus himself comes to life in it somehow, and so do the people I will address.

It is tempting to preach a passage before it has fully come to life. It's not that hard, really. You can lay out a solid exegetical outline, explain key words, colorize with good illustrations, but the sermon is too lightweight. Not so much because it is trite, but because it isn't full. Did you ever see an actor on a stage pick up a suitcase, and you just knew there was nothing in the suitcase, even though he leaned into it? He just can't fake the weight, and you begin to doubt the actor. A sermon is like that.

In the Old Testament there were priestly carriers. When Israel moved, priests carried all the parts of the Tabernacle. No trucks or carts. Just ordinary, white-clad men hefting the holy weight of God's household goods. Think of the glory of that weight, the honor of that carrying. They were like anti-pallbearers. Instead of dead weight they carried Israel's life.

The Hebrew word for *glory* (*kabod*) carries the connotation of weight. The glory of God is heavy. I get psyched to preach as I feel the heft of the weighty glory of a text of Scripture. Jesus himself is alive in this Word. In preaching we share something with those priestly forebears who carried the Ark of God's glory ahead of Israel. And some Sundays, it is as though we step into a river bearing that holy burden of a sermon, and the water parts for the people of God. The prospect of carrying the weight of God's glorious Word psyches me up; it stirs my soul to preach.

Did you bring us anything?

When it comes to getting psyched to preach, the people who sit there listening pose an interesting problem. One veteran preacher I know told me he still gets sick to his stomach some Sundays with stage fright. He gets antipsyched.

I confess my problem is the opposite. I love having an audience. It isn't a bad thing exactly, but it is dangerous. Amy Winehouse, the late drug-addled rock star, once stepped on stage and shouted, "Hello, Athens!" Only she was in Belgrade. Preachers can succumb to the performer's tendency not to really care *who* is sitting out there, so long as we have an audience.

There is also the temptation to be excited about the material we're preaching without much thought about those who will receive it. We become more like the freight hauler who delivers supplies to the church. Stack up the sermon points like boxes on a hand truck, trundle them up there by the microphone, and hold out the clipboard to whomever you can nab to confirm the delivery: "I just need you to sign here, please." Something is out of whack when a preacher really just wants someone—anyone— there so he can unload the freight of his text.

But consider a different picture. A few years ago I took a trip to India. I found myself constantly wanting to tell my wife and son about what I was seeing. I took pictures mainly so they could see what I had seen. I picked out presents for them with much more relish than I would for birthdays or Christmas at home. The main reason I anticipated getting home was to tell them all about it and to show the gifts I'd been given and the treasures I'd found for them.

I can be psyched in that way about preaching. Pastors go on a kind of solitary journey each week as we prepare a sermon. Remember when Jesus said in Matthew 13:52, "Every teacher of the law who has been instructed about the kingdom of heaven is like the owner of a house who brings out of his storeroom new treasures as well as old"? We spend hours every week in that storeroom—on that journey. And on Sunday, we come back to our Christian family with pictures and stories, with gifts we've received and presents we picked out just for them. That psyches me up to preach.

I felt this energy come

Every preacher who hews to Scripture knows that there is a mysterious holy power in preaching. What we *don't* know is just how it will come through on a Sunday morning. It is no small thing, of course, simply to set a passage of the Bible before people vividly and clearly. Simply preaching Christ is powerful and more important than anything I have a right to do, no matter if anything else happens. The privilege of simply doing that energizes me on Sunday morning.

But what also psyches me up is the possibility—actually, the likelihood—that God will do something in some lives that morning all out of proportion to anything I put in or that they expect. I read recently about a college football player from Florida who happened to be nearby when a Cadillac somehow crushed the tow truck driver trying to move it. This athlete was a big guy, but he said later, "I tried to lift the car, and when I first tried, it didn't budge." (Ever had a sermon like that?) The football player continued, "I backed up. I don't know. But I felt this energy come, and I lifted it. I don't know how, but somebody pulled him from the car."

That kind of thing happens to preachers. I don't usually even know it is happening. I don't usually "feel this energy come." But for some people sitting in that congregation, a crushing burden is lifted off them, some clear beam of truth punches light into their darkness, some new righteous resolve stirs their will and love for Christ. When they tell me about it at the door, I think, "That happened here? God did that while I was preaching? Where was I?"

Believing that such a muscular, Samson-like wonder will happen this Sunday gets my blood pumping as I wait my turn in the worship service.

Preaching under the stained glass

Biblical images psyche me up to preach. Imagine being invited to preach in a great cathedral illumined by scores of stained-glass-window pictures, all of them illustrating what happens when we preach. Look, there is the sower, his cast seeds catching the light. Over there, a red-crossed medic binding up broken hearts in bandages of Christ. Here, an open-mouthed herald, his gospel scroll gripped top and bottom. Look at that window. It is Jonah stepping pale white from his whale pulpit to preach repentance and life. And look up there at another preacher—the temple builder with plumb line and rule, laying courses of gold, silver, and precious stones upon the foundation of Christ. I preach better when I take one more look at those windows before I begin.

I get up to preach like the boy opening his homemade lunch for Jesus to see. We bow our heads, and he blesses what I've brought, and when we lift our eyes there is food enough for all of us, food that started in my basket but came manna-like to everyone from the good hand of God. We eat there together with the Lord and have basketsful left over.

Then there are the dry bones. I asked a young colleague the other day, "What's the most interesting challenge you're facing these days?" "Most interesting," he asked, "or most discouraging?" He was heavyhearted about the men in his church who seemed to respond to nothing for Christ's sake. They sat there every Sunday like dry bones propped up in the pews.

I thank God that I preach to few skeletons on Sunday, but there are always some scattered among the resurrected saints in every church. They clatter into church without spiritual muscles or sinews, nerves or thoughts. We stand at the pulpit, and God whispers as he did to Ezekiel, "Son of man, can these bones live?" "I doubt it," is what I'm thinking, but dutifully I reply, "O sovereign LORD, you alone know."

So at God's command, we again "prophesy to these bones, 'Dry bones, hear the word of the LORD!'" We preach to the holy

Wind, the Breath of God, too. And some Sundays "there is a noise, a rattling sound," and they come to their feet. What is gospel preaching but that! The prospect of facing the dry bones will surely psych us *out*, but the prospect of the Breath of God blowing into them while we preach stirs me to stand again at the pulpit.

Faith

I do not trust a preacher who doesn't get psyched to preach. I don't think we have to come out of the gate with faces flushed or pumping our fists, but we need to get "souled" up if we're to do justice to the holy text and serve Christ. All this is really just another way of describing the way we feed our faith as we prepare to speak. A preacher who does not trust God that something profound will happen delivers little more than dust. Part of sermon preparation is fortifying our faith with these realities of preaching.

Years ago I read about a preacher who would virtually jump to the pulpit when it was time to preach. His surging eagerness put his listeners on notice what they were in for. I have thought of him almost every Sunday morning in the moments before I step to the pulpit—a preacher psyched to preach.

Lee Eclov is pastor of Village Church of Lincolnshire in Lake Forest, Illinois, and author of *Pastoral Graces*.

LIKING THE LECTIONARY

*How sermon preparation can change for the better
when you preach by the church calendar.*

Timothy J. Peck

For seventeen years I was an expository preacher at a mid-sized nondenominational church in California; later, after leaving pastoral ministry, I found myself increasingly drawn to liturgy. Though when guest preaching I often delivered expository sermons, on my off Sundays I slipped into a local Episcopal church just to experience the liturgy. Eventually I joined a church plant associated with the Anglican Mission in the Americas and Bishop Todd Hunter. Now I find myself preaching twice a month at that church following the *Revised Common Lectionary* (RCL). Along the way I am learning valuable lessons about lectionary preaching that build on my experience as an expository preacher.

Discovering the lectionary

A lectionary is a book that contains appointed Scripture readings for particular days coinciding with the Christian calendar. According to preaching historian Hughes Old, use of lectionaries originated in synagogues in the fourth century before Christ. By the fourth century after Christ, church leaders had adopted this Jewish practice in Christian worship. Christians have been using lectionaries for a long time.

The *RCL* is the product of the Consultation on Common Texts (CCT), an interdenominational Christian group that began meeting in 1978. Its first draft was released in 1983 and tested for six years. After considering feedback, the *RCL* was released in 1992. The *RCL* is used worldwide by English-speaking Anglicans, Lutherans, Presbyterians, Methodists, and many other denominations. Some Baptist and nondenominational churches, as well as non-English-speaking churches, also use the *RCL*.

In addition to providing a daily Bible reading cycle (the daily office), the *RCL* on a three-year cycle assigns four readings (or lessons) for each Sunday: a psalm, an Old Testament passage (sometimes two), an Epistle passage, and a Gospel passage. Year A covers Matthew, the Old Testament patriarchs, and the exodus narrative. Year *B* covers Mark and the Old Testament monarchy narrative. Year *C* covers Luke, Israel's divided kingdom, and Old Testament prophets. John is interwoven through all three cycles, especially Year *B*. Readings from Acts are substituted for the Old Testament lesson during the Easter season. The readings for the season between Pentecost and Advent provide two options for Old Testament lessons. Although the *RCL* does not include the entire Bible, the CCT committee's intent was

> *I have discovered a new depth in keeping time with the entire Christian calendar.*

for all the voices of Scripture to be heard by the church over the course of three years.

Appreciating lectionary preaching

There are many aspects of lectionary preaching to appreciate. Foremost is that it roots preaching in the broader Christian story. This is done by correlating each week's readings with the Christian calendar, especially during Advent, Epiphany, Lent, and Easter. Previously in my pastoral ministry, the only seasons I observed were Christmas and Easter. However, more recently I have discovered a new depth in keeping time with the entire Christian calendar. The Christian calendar retells the story of Jesus each year, beginning in Advent with its anticipation of Christ's coming, to Christmas with its emphasis on the incarnation, to Epiphany with its focus on Christ's revelation to the nations, to Lent with its emphasis on Christ's prelude to suffering, to Holy Week with its emphasis on his passion, to Easter with its fifty-day emphasis on resurrection including the Ascension with its focus on Christ's exaltation as our high priest, and finally to Pentecost with its focus on Christ sending the gift of the Holy Spirit to empower the church for mission.

The *RCL* assigns readings that are appropriate to each season. For instance, the fourth Sunday of Advent in Year *A* assigns the birth account of Jesus from Matthew 1:18–25. Year *B* has Luke 1:26–38, and Year *C*, Luke 1:39–55. Over three years, both nativity accounts are fully heard. On the first Sunday after Epiphany, Year *A* has Matthew's account of Jesus' baptism, Year *B* features Mark's account, and Year *C*, Luke's account. By coordinating with this calendar, the *RCL* roots our worship and preaching in the story of Jesus.

Adapting to the rhythms of *RCL* sermon preparation

Lectionary sermon preparation can be intimidating. Instead of a single passage, the preacher has four passages to study. However, my approach is essentially the same. I analyze the passages to derive my best approximation of each passage's meaning. I use the tools of grammatical analysis, word studies, background study, and commentary work. A helpful source I have discovered is the Feasting on the Word commentary series edited by David Bartlett and Barbara Brown Taylor (Westminster John Knox Press). This commentary offers theological, pastoral, exegetical, and homiletical essays on each *RCL* passage following the liturgical calendar.

Another important part of preparation is probing the connections between the passages. The CCT strategically grouped texts together during Advent, Epiphany, Lent, and Easter. Finding the threads that connect these passages enables a preacher to craft sermons that are both biblical and that honor the tapestry of the assigned texts. The CCT intentionally avoided typological reading of the Old Testament; it selected Old Testament texts that have a clear connection with the Gospel reading prescribed for the day. In the preface to the *RCL*, the CCT briefly describes its overall approach to pairing Old Testament and Gospel texts.

For example, the third Sunday in Lent in Year *A* assigns a reading from Exodus 17:1–7, a narrative of Israel's testing God in the wilderness because they had no water. Psalm 95 is also assigned, which is a later reflection on Exodus 17:1–7, with the psalmist warning new generations not to be like the exodus generation. The *RCL* is filled with these intertextual links for the preacher willing to look for them. Although the CCT doesn't elaborate on its specific reasons for pairing texts, many of these connections are explored in the Feasting on the Word commentaries.

Another kind of connection between passages is a common metaphor. For instance, the third Sunday in Lent of Year A lists the following texts: Exodus 17:1–7, Psalm 95, Romans 5:1–11, and John 4:5–42. As previously mentioned, there is an intertextual link between the passages from Exodus and the Psalms; beyond that, a common metaphor joins the readings. Exodus and John both contain narratives about water: in Exodus the water gushing from the rock, and in John the living water offered by Jesus to the Samaritan woman at the well. Similarly, Paul uses a water verb in Romans 5:5, "poured out." Water is a common metaphor that thematically unites these texts.

The CCT does not intertextually pair texts during the season between Pentecost and Advent. Instead, the texts during this season (Ordinary Time) follow a semicontinuous pattern relatively autonomous from each other.

When constructing a lectionary sermon, the preacher must decide how to design it. One strategy is to preach all four texts, spending time on each one and crafting transitional statements that use the textual connections to progress. Another is to select one of the readings, basing the sermon primarily on that text and weaving into that explanation insights gleaned from the other passages. This is especially appropriate on special days, when one text encapsulates the theme on that particular day. Still another strategy, particularly appropriate for the season between Pentecost and Advent, is to select one section of the lectionary readings, such as the patriarchal narrative or the Gospel, and preach continuously through that book each week.

Preaching from the *RCL* has been a great adventure. It builds on my previous training as an expository preacher by helping me stay rooted in the Christian story. Preaching the *RCL* also forces me to grapple with texts that I would not normally be drawn to, often finding hidden insights that I would have missed otherwise.

Timothy J. Peck is director of the chapel and a lecturer in the school of theology at Azusa Pacific University, Azusa, California. He preaches regularly at Christ Our King Church in Azusa.

WRITING A GOOD MESSAGE
IN A BAD WEEK

What to do when you can't invest your normal study time.

Scott Wenig

For even the most diligent and disciplined preacher, those weeks come in which time for sermon preparation is short. What should we do?

How we use the time we have for sermon preparation is the single-most important human factor in the effectiveness of the sermon. Obviously, if he so chooses, God can take anything we offer and empower it to produce Pentecost! But more often than not it is the quality of our preparation, regardless of how stressed we may be, which makes the difference between poverty and potency in the pulpit. I would offer the following suggestions for sermon preparation to time-squeezed pastors.

Work during peak hours

For those who feel they're most efficient early in the day, I suggest giving three to four hours each morning to sermon preparation. But if you're like a pastor friend of mine who comes alive at eleven at night, then study as much as you can after the rest of your family has gone to bed.

My guess is that the average pastor, who must lead meetings, do hospital visitation, provide some pastoral care, and be available for staff and other types of counseling, has at most twelve to fifteen hours each week for sermon preparation. Those hours must be stewarded wisely, which means working during the time of day (or night) when you can give your best to the preparation process.

Get ahead

This may sound unrealistic to the time-squeezed, but if you can find a way to get a day or two ahead, you'll be pleasantly surprised to discover how much this can improve the quality of your preaching. A number of years ago, social psychologists studied people of a creative bent—artists, musicians, writers, and poets—to discover the secret of their success. They discovered that the vast majority of those they studied seemed to work intuitively in a ten-day creative cycle. For preachers to become homiletically creative, this means starting some of the exegetical or sermon work for the *following week's* sermon on Thursday of the current week.

Obviously this takes discipline, but when it's done, the rewards roll forth: more time to think about the

> *How we use the time we have for sermon preparation is generally the single-most important human factor in the effectiveness of the sermon.*

particular passage or theme, more opportunities to collect current illustrations, and more time given to relevant application. I've discovered that if I'm a bit ahead in the process, it actually goes faster once I start because I've given myself more time to meditate on the message and how it might come together.

Draw from previous sermons

When I was in seminary, one of my professors preached a sterling sermon in chapel that had a profound impact on a number of the students, myself included. Afterward, one of the students asked him, "How long did it take you to prepare that message?" His answer has never left me: "Three hours and thirty years." As an experienced pastor and a person who had lived some life, he had a great depository of material to draw from. This saved him innumerable hours in the sermon-writing process.

If you find yourself in a situation where you have only five hours to put together a sermon, don't be afraid to pull some things out of the file and rework them. If it's true that some of your sermons should go into the shredder, it's also true that some of them can and should be used again.

If you are redoing an old sermon, devote the majority of the available time to making the illustrations current and sharpening the applications. Since the original sermon was solid, you need not tamper with the basic content. Moreover, while I encourage preaching without notes, I would never hesitate, under the constraints of time, to take some notes with me into the pulpit.

Borrow ethically

The operative word here is *ethical*. We must be both honest and careful about what we use and how much we use from others, especially when we're time strapped. One way to do so ethically is to "footnote" the other preacher in your sermon. For example, I recently preached a sermon on envy in which I borrowed some material from a book by a very prominent preacher who happens to be a personal favorite of mine. I had no reservations about giving him public credit for his insights on the topic, and doing so made the sermon stronger and helped me stay ethical.

Another way to avoid pulpit plagiarism is to take the ideas and illustrations of other preachers and use them as a catalyst for finding those in our own experience. For example, a preacher once used a humorous personal experience to communicate clearly our tendency to deceive ourselves into thinking that we're better than we really are. It was so powerful that it motivated me to look into my life to see if there were any situations where I had done the same thing. Fortunately, there were, and I used one of those as an introduction to a sermon on our need for a Savior. This technique not only saves us time, it also enables our messages to come out of the reality of our own lives.

Use all the available homiletical resources at your disposal. While there is danger in borrowing, it's an enormous blessing to have so many legitimate and available resources at hand.

Get up earlier

Since we're all pressed for time and cannot create more, we must use more efficiently what we already possess. Getting up fifteen minutes earlier on the days of our workweek and then an hour on both Saturday and Sunday gives us three extra hours per week. I don't think it's realistic to ask more of ourselves than this since we're already strapped. But if we dedicate these few additional hours to prayer and sermon preparation, in due course our preaching will really benefit. Minimally, this allows us to invest more time in both biblical exegesis and meditation with the Lord.

But what if you're able to add only one extra hour, not three? How should it be best invested? My suggestion is to use that extra sixty minutes rehearsing the sermon's delivery and asking God for his anointing.

Regardless of the amount of time at our disposal, we can prepare to the best of our ability given those constraints and preach in a Spirit-filled fashion.

Scott Wenig is associate professor of applied theology at Denver Seminary in Denver, Colorado.

14

FACEBOOK™ SERMON PREP

A late adopter discovers a surprisingly useful tool.

Bill White

For years friends pestered me to sign up for Facebook™, the social networking Web site that keeps you up to date with people you know well or not so well. Since I wasn't that interested in the movie preferences of my ninth grade lab partner or in the gossip from my mother's third cousin, I figured, "Why spend precious time online that I desperately need for face-to-face relationships?"

Then, on a whim, I signed up for Facebook™. I have been surprised by how useful it has been as a ministry tool, especially for preaching.

Over the past four months as I've mentioned being on Facebook™, more than 35 percent of our congregation have become "friends." I've also added as "friends" a couple of dozen folks who have dropped out of church altogether, plus a number of unchurched people (from my kids' soccer teams and school, mostly). I now have a new level of interaction with these people, which I'm finding very helpful. Here's how:

Understanding the hearts of my people

For a recent sermon series about fasting, I must have read a hundred comments about what our people were learning, struggling with, and giving up. Each week I could spend ten minutes on Facebook™ and read a couple of dozen comments about people's experiences, which helped me calibrate where the church was on our journey. Comments like this helped me prepare the coming week's sermon: "I feel a sense of urgency to learn something. Problem is that I'm so concentrated on not breaking the fast (I've slipped a few times) that I might be missing the point. . . ."

> *Each week I could spend ten minutes on Facebook™ and read a couple of dozen comments about people's experiences.*

Understanding the hearts of the unchurched

Facebook™ keeps me connected with people outside the church with whom I'd otherwise have little contact. I keep their struggles in mind as I prepare messages. Just this week, I read this status update from a FB friend who dropped out of church a decade ago:

"If you pray, do me a favor and pray for me. I'm having a really rough time right now. Even though I don't show it, I'm dying inside. I don't know who to talk to, and I'm just overwhelmed with hurt and everything else. I just feel like I need to let go, but I don't know how."

Bringing people to church

Besides praying for this woman, I also contacted her and invited her to an evangelistic service we were having that evening—and she came! Well, I should say, she stood outside while another leader and I talked with her. She didn't actually step inside. But it was a huge step for her.

Besides her, six other unchurched FB friends whom I've personally invited have shown up to Sunday services.

Generating sermon material

A story we used at our Easter services was one that popped up on FB from a lady from church. It just showed up in the daily flow of postings. I grabbed it and used it. This week I tried something more intentional. The sermon needed an illustration about extending forgiveness. So on Monday, in my status field, I posted a request for stories. I received seven forgiveness stories in response! Yesterday one of our college students videotaped one of those people sharing her story, and we're showing it on Sunday—tears and all.

Extending the sermon's impact

Recently one of our leaders posted "Great sermon!" on my Facebook™ page, so I wrote back asking why she felt led to say that. That led to a significant online conversation about the spiritual growth that was sparked by how the preached word intersected her life. After its delivery I've also posted quotes/testimonies from my sermon and had many people connect with that material. Once I even published an entire manuscript of one of our more controversial messages. In response I had some really good interaction over the Scriptures and their meaning, an interaction that many people followed as it unfolded online.

I'm still new to Facebook™, so I'm still learning. Besides the benefits, there are plenty of dangers—including wasting time and inappropriate content. Just like any other form of relationship building, Facebook™ takes time, energy, and discretion. But it's a useful tool for preaching.

Bill White is outreach pastor at Emmanuel Reformed Church in Paramount, California.

PREPARING MORE THAN
ONE SERMON PER WEEK

*How to maximize your preparation time
and keep sermon quality high.*

Steve Mathewson

If your church or ministry setting requires you to prepare more than one sermon a week, how can you prepare an additional sermon after pouring everything into the first one? It's the challenge you face if your church has a Sunday night or midweek service in addition to your primary weekend worship service(s). Let me state the question from another angle: if it takes all your time and energy just to produce one quality sermon a week, how can you hope to prepare two better-than-mediocre sermons week in and week out?

Admittedly, it's been a while since I've faced this challenge. I currently prepare only one sermon a week, and I still have my hands full! But I've faced this challenge in previous pastorates, and I have five suggestions for making it work.

Prioritize

First, you must prioritize. Spend most of your time preparing the sermon for your primary worship service(s), and spend less time preparing for the secondary preaching opportunity. This is a strategic move born of a desire to give your people your very best. Usually there will be fewer people at the secondary events. This does not mean that you should settle for a sloppy, half-baked sermon. But if you simply divide your time equally, you may end up with two mediocre sermons. My theory is that spending 80 percent of your time on your primary sermon and 20 percent on the secondary one(s) can actually produce two compelling sermons. Spending less time on the secondary one will force you down a different creative process and path.

> *If you simply divide your preparation time equally, you may end up with two mediocre sermons.*

Recycle

Second, feel free to recycle. A good sermon is worth preaching twice, especially if you rework it the second time around. Normally, I'll let at least four years pass before bringing a sermon back—longer if I'm going to reuse a series. If you reuse a sermon or a series in a secondary preaching setting, make sure to interact with at least one new commentary or resource when you rework it, so that you are forced to do some fresh thinking. Also, change an illustration or the sermon's structure. Make sure to reread the text a few times and pray through it. You don't have to duplicate all the exegetical work you did before. Just build on it! God's Spirit will honor both your previous work and your new work.

Expand

Third, expand themes or material from your primary sermon for use in the secondary setting. Often, studying for your primary sermon will yield more material than you can use at one time, so you should feel free to use it in your secondary sermon. For example, I preached last Sunday on Proverbs 3:1–12. If I had a secondary opportunity, I would pursue one of several options. I might preach on Hebrews 12:4–13, since it offers a "sermon" on Proverbs 3:11–12. Or I might develop the topic of God's guidance, which emerges from Proverbs 3:5–6. I could develop this issue in another sermon, which would have a more topical/theological, rather than expositional, flow.

Apply

Fourth, use the secondary setting to wrestle with application. In my opinion, North American Christianity does not devote enough time to application. As a result, some churches schedule a discussion forum after a worship service or during adult education time. To counter this tendency, devote the secondary setting to a brief recap of the sermon, and then let people ask questions or suggest what it will look like to flesh out the teaching of the text in everyday life situations. Urge people to think specifically. Vague application leads to vague Christian living.

Recruit

Finally, use secondary settings to let others in the church exercise and develop their gifts. Reserve these opportunities for other pastoral staff members or for preachers in training.

I hope one of these approaches, or a combination of them, will help you make the best use of the time you devote to preaching the Word.

Steve Mathewson is pastor of the Evangelical Free Church of Libertyville, Illinois, and teaches preaching for the doctoral programs at Denver Seminary and Western Seminary, and the master of divinity program at Trinity Evangelical Divinity School. He is author of *The Art of Preaching Old Testament Narrative* (Baker Academic).

How I Prepare a Sermon:
Interviews

All preachers have their signature method of sermon preparation. Their method reflects their personalities, mentors, and what they have picked up from other preachers here and there. In the following interviews and articles, we hope that you find a few ideas to add to your own signature style of creating sermons that change people's lives.

Timothy Keller

Tell us about your planning process for preaching.

Every June I flesh out all of my sermon topics, titles, and texts for the coming year, and then I send them off to my music director and other associate preachers. During vacation and study time in the summer, I read books on the themes I'll be treating in the sermons during the coming year. At the end of the summer, my reading leads me to revise the list of topics and texts, and then we are good to go.

What does your weekly sermon preparation look like?

Ten days before the Sunday that I will preach a sermon, I spend three hours doing basic exegesis and outlining. The Friday morning before I preach the sermon, I spend five hours writing a first draft of the sermon. On Saturday morning I spend four hours writing a second draft. That Saturday night I spend another two to three hours writing a third draft. With each draft I shorten and streamline the message. I then get up very early on Sunday morning and spend two hours reading it through several times, essentially memorizing all the basic points and subpoints.

I pastor a large church and have a large staff, so I give special prominence to preparing the sermon. I give it fifteen to eighteen hours a week. I would not advise younger ministers to spend that much time on sermon preparation, however. The main way to become a good preacher is to preach a lot and to spend tons of time in people work. That's how you become something more than a Bible commentator; you become a flesh-and-blood preacher. When I was without a large staff, I spent six to eight hours in sermon preparation.

Which tools do you find most helpful?

I use *BibleWorks™* software and lots of commentaries.

How do you generate sermon ideas?

It's a great mistake to pit pastoral care and leadership against preaching preparation. Many of my preaching ideas come to me as I am talking to, exhorting, counseling, evangelizing, and shepherding people. It is only through working with people that you become the preacher you need to be—someone who knows sin, how the heart works, what people's struggles are, and so on. To some degree, pastoral care and leadership *are* sermon preparation! They prepare the preacher and not just the sermon.

What devotional material do you use for your personal growth?

I use a version of M'Cheyne's reading calendar, reading the Bible in its entirety every year. I also follow the traditional daily office, and I read and pray all the psalms every month. I use older versions of the *Book of Common Prayer* for many of my prayers.

Finally, what are your goals as you shape a sermon?

Preaching should be biblical, clear for the mind, practical for the will, vivid for the heart, warm, forceful, and Christocentric. You should always preach Christ and the gospel from every text!

Timothy Keller is pastor of Redeemer Presbyterian Church in New York, New York. He is also cofounder and vice president of the Gospel Coalition and author of *The Reason for God*.

Steve Mathewson

Are there any key questions you normally answer, or paths of thought you typically take, as you study a text and write the sermon?

I've been mentored by Haddon Robinson, so I am big on asking two questions to determine the main idea. The first is, what is this passage talking about? The second is, what is this passage saying about what it is talking about? These questions help me identify what Haddon calls the subject and complement of the main idea.

Sometimes if I'm struggling to identify the big idea, I will also ask, what is the vision of God? That is, what aspect of God's character is prominent in this text (such as God's power, mercy, vengeance, role as a Father). Then I also ask, what is the depravity factor? That is, what is the sin that works against what God is doing or requiring in this passage? Again, I got these questions from Haddon Robinson. Bryan Chapell also speaks of the second one, calling it the fallen condition focus. Once I have the big idea in place, I ask three questions about the main idea as it relates to the biblical writer and my audience:

- What does this mean? (explanation)

- Is it true? (validation)

- How does this relate to our lives? (application)

With regard to the writer, I am trying to figure out if the writer developed the idea primarily by explaining, validating, or applying—or a combination of these. With regard to my listeners, I am trying to determine what details and ideas from the text need to be explained, which need to be validated, and which need to be applied. This helps me determine what I include in my sermon and what I leave on the cutting-room floor.

There's another question from Haddon that I will use when wrestling with application: if someone were sitting in my office discussing a problem, and I turned to this text for the answer, what is the problem that would prompt me to turn to this text to give them spiritual direction?

What schedule routine do you follow in sermon preparation?

Because I take Fridays off, I begin my sermon prep on Monday. I have about three hours before our staff meeting, so I read the passage in its original language and do a mechanical layout if I'm in epistles or legal literature. Then I will make observations about the FACTS:

- form (literary genre)

- art (imagery, literary devices)

- context (literary and historical-cultural)

- terms (key words, repeated words, unfamiliar words)

- structure (how the argument flows)

If I am preaching from a narrative, I look for the ACTS:

- action (plot)

- characters

- talking (dialogue, key statements made by the characters)

- setting (literary and historical-cultural)

Finally I write out a preliminary statement of what I think the main idea is.

On Monday afternoon I begin reading three or four of the best commentaries. I continue this on Tuesday morning and refine my understanding of the idea.

By Wednesday morning I think about how I am going to preach this. I begin working on a preliminary preaching idea. I run this by a preaching planning team (composed of staff members) on Wednesday afternoon.

Then on Thursday I refine the outline and fill in the details. I usually prepare a detailed outline with a few sections manuscripted.

Friday is my day off. On Saturday I return to the outline and read through it, sometimes making minor revisions. I talk my way through the sermon—either in my office or in a more deliberate rehearsal in our worship center. I do this a couple of times and always on Saturday night to lock it into my mind, since I preach with minimal or no notes.

Steve Mathewson is pastor of the Evangelical Free Church of Libertyville, Illinois, and teaches preaching for the doctoral programs at Denver Seminary and Western Seminary, and the master of divinity program at Trinity Evangelical Divinity School. He is author of *The Art of Preaching Old Testament Narrative* (Baker Academic).

135

Mark Driscoll

Tell us about your preparation process.

I prayerfully choose a book of the Bible that bites me and plan on spending months, and sometimes years, studying that book of the Bible in preparation to preach it. A book like Genesis will take me more than a thousand hours of work to study, write commentary for, and preach.

I continually pray for the Holy Spirit to teach me his Word as I am studying the Scripture. No amount of theological training can overcome the deficit of a preacher who is not led by the Holy Spirit to understand and proclaim the very words that he inspired.

As I study, I wrestle with tough texts as Jacob wrestled Jesus. I find that preaching tough texts such as gender roles, the flood, and hell are much like driving a car into a steep curve. If you hit the brakes in fear, you will lose control, but if you accelerate into the tough turns, gravity actually slingshots you through smoothly. Momentum and authority come through accelerating into tough texts in study and then driving the church through them in the pulpit.

As I study Scripture, I steep in the verses, phrases, words, and pictures that bite like tea flavoring in hot water. Too often the principles of Scripture are preached when the images and word pictures are far more impacting and memorable. For this reason other movements have even co-opted the biblical images so that a dove now represents peace and not the Holy Spirit, and a rainbow represents gay rights and not the flood in which God killed people for sinning. I find that sermons become memorable if the images in the Scriptures can be drilled into the imagination of people. Perhaps the master at this was Charles Haddon Spurgeon, who would not just describe a scene of Scripture, but actually put you in it through your imagination.

Only after I have spent considerable time in the naked text do I check my studies with trusted teachers to ensure that I have not come to heretical conclusions. I try not to pick up the commentaries until I have had many months in the Scripture I am preaching to ensure that I do not get lazy or simply rely on another man's walk with God. I will read it repeatedly in multiple translations and read every decent commentary from every theological persuasion I can find to examine the book from every angle.

I live what I learn, teach it to my family, and spend a lot of time repenting of sin and seeking to obey God's Word by the grace he provides. Much of my sermon is then simply explaining what the Scripture says, how that has changed my life, and how that is causing transformation in my family and those people I live in community with. In this way I hope to exemplify to my church coming under Scripture by talking about my own sins and flaws so that they see me struggling through Scripture and not just preaching my tidy answers at the end of my studies. Because of this, my sermons are long, anywhere from an hour to an hour and a half.

What methods of research do you use, and which tools do you find most helpful?

I find myself continually coming back to five questions that shape every one of my sermons:

1. What does Scripture say? To answer this we need to check translations, do our word studies, and find out exactly what words best convey the meaning of Scripture.

2. What does Scripture mean? Here we need to interpret what is said, which requires commentaries, cultural background studies, and so on. At this phase John Glynn's *Commentary and Reference Survey* is a must-have for every preacher and teacher, as he rates all of the best commentaries and other reference material on various books of the Bible and theological topics.

3. Why do we resist this truth? Here we are assuming that people will not simply embrace God's truth but fight it with their thoughts and actions because they are sinners who, as Romans 1:18 says, suppress the truth. So we attempt to predetermine their objections and resistance so that we can answer them and remove their resistance to get them to embrace God's truth for their life. This part of the sermon must be confrontational and often ends up in people walking out, standing up to argue, and sending nasty e-mails, all of which indicates you've hit a nerve, as God wants you to. The real fight begins at this point, and a preacher needs to come with his hands up looking for an opening, much like a boxer.

4. Why does this matter? We need to connect all that we have said to a missional purpose for our lives, families,

church, and ultimately God's glory. Something may be true, but if people do not also find it important, they tend not to act on it. On this point I like to connect Scripture to the character of God, the nature of the gospel, our mission in our city, and the quality of our lives both individually and collectively as a city of God within our city.

5. How is Jesus the hero? The Bible is one story in which Jesus is the hero. Therefore, to properly teach/preach the Bible, we have to continually lift him up as the hero; any sermon in which the focus is not on the person and work of Jesus will lack spiritual authority and power because the Holy Spirit will not bless the teaching of any hero other than Jesus.

What other advice can you offer to preachers?

First, junk your notes and go with the Ghost. Some years ago I gave up trying to manuscript or outline my sermons. Now I focus on knowing the Scriptures I am preaching, spending many hours in prayer, meditation, and repentance through the Scriptures, and being filled with the power of God the Ghost. Then I just get up, and with a few scribbled notes in my margins I preach as God leads and trust that God will direct my words, and he always does.

Second, plug everything into your pulpit. I have gone to writing long commentaries on books of the Bible I am preaching with study tips, small group questions, family devotional questions. We also have our children's ministry and small group ministry follow the teaching from the pulpit, so the whole church is studying and learning together to ensure focus and unity.

Third, preach Jesus. Jesus' name should be spoken repeatedly throughout a sermon so that it is clear which God you are speaking of. Jesus should be the hero of every sermon, the answer to every question, and the hope for every person. Jesus promised that if he is lifted up he would draw people, and the key to church growth is the exaltation of Jesus.

Fourth, preach Jesus some more.

Fifth, give your sermons away. Some years ago we started putting the sermons online for free MP3 downloads. Today, with podcasting, we are seeing more than 1 million free downloads a year of the sermons. The Web is the new front door, and many people will visit your church through your Web site long before they attend a church event. Also, many people like to catch up on past teachings, forward pertinent sermons to their friends, and listen to teaching while they drive to work, cook their meals, and weed their garden. By giving the sermon away for free, the preacher's ministry can continue for years into the future to a much broader audience than on a Sunday.

Sixth, after you've preached, let it go. Don't listen to your sermons over and over, beating yourself up. Once you've preached a sermon, let it be a finished work and move on. Passion, courage, and boldness are keys to preaching that simply cannot exist in someone who is too analytical or critical of themselves, so lighten up, have fun, and let it fly in Jesus' name.

Mark Driscoll is preaching pastor and cofounder of Mars Hill Church in Seattle, Washington, and coauthor of *Doctrine* (Crossway).

Justin Buzzard

Several years ago as a staff pastor, I developed the following process for writing my sermons in three stages, requiring a total of fifteen hours. I'm a church planter now, so this has become the ideal, considering real-world demands.

Tilling the soil: study the text and structure the sermon

This stage requires five hours, and I do it on the Monday thirteen days before I preach.

1. **Study the text.** Pause to pray over this sermon, then enjoy the creation process with a heart of faith. In recent weeks I've been jotting down ideas for this sermon on a prep sheet, but this, now, is the official start of sermon prep. Record notes on a prep sheet. View sermon prep as a vital piece of my discipleship; Jesus has called me to preach for my own sanctification and joy. Beware of idolatry in my heart: What's ruling me as I prepare this sermon—Jesus and his gospel or some idol of performance?

Note the immediate context of the text. Determine the text's genre and begin pestering the text with historical and literary questions. All knowledge is covenantal—meant for obedience—what is this text meant to do? Read the text many times to determine its flow; read other translations; examine the text in its original language. Are there any significant differences? Is there unusual or significant grammar? Are there words worthy of study? Are there any important historical or cultural matters to explain? What stands out to me? Consider memorizing the text over the next two weeks.

Write a complete-sentence exegetical outline of the text.

Think through the biblical theology connections. How does this text fit in with the overall storyline of the Bible? What gaps does it fill? What hinges on this passage? Consider using a crucial cross-reference or two. Determine the text's relation to Jesus: is it predictive, preparatory, resultant, or reflective of Jesus? Identify the gospel pointers. What does the text say about man's redemptive need or problem and God's redemptive provision?

Get to the gospel and Jesus via

- theme resolution (every biblical theme finds its resolution in the gospel)

- law fulfillment (every biblical law finds its fulfillment in Jesus)

- story completion (every biblical story finds its climax in Jesus)

- need met (every human need finds its answer in the gospel)

- problem solved (every human problem finds its ultimate solution in the gospel)

- contrast (many biblical passages can be contrasted with the good news found in Jesus)

- symbol/type fulfillment (the many symbols and "types" in Scripture are fulfilled in Jesus)

Think through the systematic theology connections in the text. How can I use this passage to make people more theologically alert?

Write out the exegetical thesis of the text in a single sentence. Test the sentence subject to see if it's too narrow or too broad. Sentence complements (predicates) could later serve as main points in the sermon.

Study about three of the best commentaries. Aim for a mix of technical, preaching, and devotional commentaries. Read or listen to at least one sermon on the text. Less is more; don't take in too much input.

II. **Determine the purpose, application, aims, and thesis of the sermon.** Why is this text here? So what? How can this text nourish my sheep?

Solve people's problems with the text or the gospel. Climb the abstraction ladder. How has this text been addressing my life? What do I want people to know, feel, do from this text? Write a purpose statement for the sermon.

Write a sharp, twenty-first-century-worded sermon thesis, of fifteen words or less. Try including both doctrine and application in this sentence. Say it in a sentence. What is the burden, the claim, of the text that's beginning to burn in me? This sentence doesn't always have to surface in the sermon, but most of the time it will.

III. **Outline the sermon.** Question the text about the thesis to help erect a focused outline. Have a clear plotline for the sermon; think of the sermon as a story. A three-point outline often works best. Decide on the approach of the outline: deductive (thesis stated up front) or inductive (question/problem/tension/mystery presented in the beginning that moves toward the thesis/resolution near the ending). Vary between deductive and inductive text reading. Vary where to place prayer in the sermon. Sometimes hide the outline when preaching. Be a sticky communicator; make sermons Simple, Unexpected, Concrete, Credible, Emotional, Storied (SUCCESs, as taught in *Made to Stick* by Chip and Dan Heath).

Write my sermon outline using complete sentences and twenty-first-century language for main points/movements and subpoints/movements.

Write an engaging introduction that surfaces need, that makes people say, "I need to hear this." Use a provocative question, human-interest story, simple assertion, startling statement, a catalog of information, or create a conflict/problem. Depending on the approach of the outline, the introduction could set up the whole thesis, just the subject of the thesis, or just the first point. Go after people's sweet spot with the introduction.

End with a conclusion that either (1) serves as the last main point, (2) reviews, (3) returns full circle to the introduction, (4) creates a climax, (5) sounds a call to mission or new possibilities, (6) exalts Christ, or (7) demonstrates the sermon in action. Seek the natural stopping place.

Planting the seed: make a hybrid draft of the sermon

My second stage of preparation requires four hours, and I do this on Wednesday eleven days out from the day I will preach.

Make a hybrid draft of the sermon, which is more than a detailed outline and less than a manuscript rough draft. It fills out, details, and sharpens the movement of the sermon, preparing for the final draft next week.

Provide supporting material to the outline and plug in material from the prep sheet that serves the thesis of the sermon. Less is more; disregard notes that don't serve where God is leading me with this sermon.

Use complete sentences throughout most of the draft. Use humor. Determine whether I need to explain, illustrate, or apply the main points.

I. **Explain.** Preach to Christians and non-Christians every week. Explain and prove the points by fleshing out unspoken premises. Give as much biblical information as the people need to understand the passage, and no more, then move on to illustration or application. Explain to believers and unbelievers. Anticipate listeners' questions (use questions to transition and set up points). Consider addressing a "defeater belief." Expose and challenge people's idols—personal, cultural, religious. Show how true resolution, perhaps a third way, is found only in your text. Unless a quote is excellent, put it in my own words. As I explain, make it my greater focus to proclaim.

II. **Illustrate.** Plug in illustrations that tap the five senses. Make biblical principles immediately tangible. Freshly incarnate biblical truth each week. Aim to illustrate each main point. Preach images. Entice with illustrations. Restore wonder in people. Live on the lookout for sermon illustrations; turn life into a workshop for preaching.

III. **Apply.** Add application under each main point or near the sermon's close. Make biblical principles immediately practical. Personally counsel the people with the text. Motivate by grace—feed people's faith; show that God is for them. Write out applications that are concrete and specific. Is there a command to obey? A promise to claim? A sin to avoid? A warning to heed? A fact to believe? A truth to ponder? What does this text say to the Christian, non-Christian, and immature Christian in the church? Consider setting up an application trajectory in the introduction. Reveal my own life and how it intersects with this text.

Look at the world through the lens of the sermon. Believe the truth and practice the behavior I will preach. Talk to other people about the message; give mini-sermons that test out the message. Let these conversations edit the sermon. Transform procrastination into rehearsal.

Get away from the sermon. Do other things, and more sermon clarity will come. Add good ideas to the draft.

Germination: write a final draft of the sermon

The third stage requires six hours on the Thursday three days out.

Rewrite the whole sermon in one sitting using a printout of the hybrid draft. Writing in one sitting ingrains in me the flow of the sermon. Write like it's an emergency. Make believe I have to preach it once six hours is up. Keep moving. Kill perfectionism. Trust my instincts. Write like I talk; talk the message out loud as I write. Don't manuscript everything; keep many portions of the draft in bullet-point form (when I know it, use bullet points; when the idea is fuzzy, write it out—I can reduce later if needed). Repeat key words; employ repetition. Be clear. Be simple. Be colorful and memorable. Underline one key phrase or sentence per paragraph as a visual cue. Pray as I write. Enjoy the process.

Know the ideal length of the draft for comfortable pace and timing, which for me is nine pages, 1.5 spacing, Times Roman font size 14, totaling 2,350 words (biblical text included). That results in a thirty-five- to forty-minute sermon.

Keep looking at life via the sermon, preaching the sermon to myself, talking the sermon out with others, but stay away from the manuscript until Saturday night. Internalize the sermon. Visualize the sermon.

Read the sermon Saturday night before bed and Sunday morning immediately after waking up. Read it repeatedly and rapidly—reading to get the flow and main movements, not the sentences. Make last minute adjustments. Consider doing a rough, fast-forward run-through of the sermon in the pulpit on Sunday morning to get a sense of pace, gesturing, movement. Don't spend much time on any of this. Give the sermon to God. Trust God and his Word.

Justin Buzzard is pastor of Garden City Church in San Jose, California. He is author of *Date Your Wife* (Crossway).

Ligon Duncan

Tell us about your sermon preparation process.

Before I begin planning a sermon, I look at the book of the Bible and break it into pericopes. Those pericopes change from time to time, though, depending upon how much I'm trying to bite off in the course of an exposition.

My sermon preparation process entails reading the text multiple times in different English versions, but my nose is in the original text from the very beginning. I use *BibleWorks™* from start to finish (with its wonderful tools, lexicons, morphology resources, and so on), checking the Greek, Hebrew, or Aramaic background to the text (looking for words and phrases that are especially important to the biblical author). I prefer an essentially literal English translation, but even with that aid, I want to make sure that I'm paying attention to the vocabulary and word order of the original, so that I don't allow the English to drive my understanding and exposition in an unhelpful (and inaccurate) direction.

After I've read the passage numerous times and have a feel for it in the original, I try to outline the text in my mind. In other words, I try to organize the passage as best as I can just from reading the propositional flow of the passage.

Once the text is outlined, I read about fifteen to twenty commentaries on that particular passage. I sift through those commentaries looking for three things: (1) key exegetical or expositional insights, (2) key application insights, and (3) key illustrative insights.

I will then modify my outline based upon the input of my reading of all the commentators. Sometimes I think that their outline is better than mine. Sometimes I don't. Either way, I come up with a final outline for the passage both exegetically and homiletically. That is, I create an outline that represents the flow of the passage, and then I turn it into a homiletical statement so that I'm not simply stating what the text says, but what God, through the writer of Scripture and that particular passage, is laying claim on hearers to believe, to do, to think, to desire, or to be.

Finally, I highlight the points that I'm going to be able to cover in the passage. Some have three points, some five, some seven, some twenty-three. Then I try to decide how much time I have to actually preach that material.

What are your personal study habits?

I carry around commentaries in my bag and read them at stoplights, at airports, in cars on the way to lunch, and while I'm waiting to pick up the children at school. I tend to do sermon preparation in the morning and late at night. I probably keep seven to ten books going at a given time outside of my sermon reading.

What research tools do you find most helpful?

I constantly use the *BibleWorks*™ software program. It's on my computer screen from the beginning of my sermon preparation to the very end. I use its Bible dictionaries, its word searches, its lexicons, its text analysis tools, and more. I regularly use the various versions of the Old and New Testaments.

I use a number of Bible dictionaries and encyclopedias in various parts of sermon planning—especially if I am working on introductory material. Say I'm getting ready to do a series on the book of Numbers; I'm going to look at Old Testament Bible dictionaries and Bible handbooks, looking for helps in doing overall outlines of the biblical book.

What general advice can you offer to other preachers?

The truth of the Bible is the most exciting truth in all the world, and so, while our job is not to make it exciting, our presentation of it ought not to diminish the excitement, practicality, and power of the truth of God's Word. We always ought to aim to do justice to the power and practicality of whatever passage we're preaching.

We should never look outside of the passage for something that will make the sermon especially attractive and compelling to the people; the Word of God itself is compelling and attractive to those who are regenerate. And it is compelling and attractive to those upon whom the Holy Spirit is performing his convicting and converting work. If we have to go to something outside of the Word, then what we're trying to do is make the Scripture compelling and attractive to the natural man, which hates the Word of God, and thereby we starve the sheep and cut off the one hope of salvation to the unconverted.

What devotional material do you use for your personal growth?

I use a lot of different devotional helps. I read Charles H. Spurgeon's *Morning and Evening* over and over again. M'Cheyne's

Bible reading program is still very helpful (four chapters a day, in order to read through the Bible in a year—the New Testament and Psalms twice and the Old Testament just once). I have recently been using William Still's *Through the Year with William Still,* which Banner of Truth produced. I read a lot of nineteenth-century Communion preparation books, like Edward Bickersteth's *A Treatise on Prayer* or *A Treatise on Preparation for the Lord's Supper.* I also read a lot of Puritan and Scottish Reformation material, like Thomas Boston and Thomas Brooks. A friend recently recommended that I try reading one sermon a day. To that end, I'm reading Mark Dever's marvelous two-volume set, *The Message of the Old Testament: Promises Made* and *The Message of the New Testament: Promises Kept* (both by Crossway). I just stumbled across a little gem called *A Consuming Fire: The Piety of Alexander Whyte,* by Michael Haykin and Joel Beeke (Reformation Heritage Books). It is excellent—convicting and encouraging.

How do you generate sermon ideas?

I typically preach through Bible books, so that keeps me from having to generate sermon ideas, because the next passage generates what will be preached the next week. That having been said, along with my preaching colleague, Derek Thomas (our minister of teaching), I do at least one topical-expository series a year—almost always at Christmastime and sometimes during the summer.

Naturally the Christmas series is incarnation-centric. Sometimes it is working through the libretto of Handel's *Messiah* and preaching those texts while the choir sings the corresponding chorus. Sometimes I work my way through the messianic texts of the Old Testament. Sometimes I preach through Luke's nativity narratives.

Apart from Christmas, I may take a look at the theological emphases of Nicaea and Chalcedon on the person of Christ. Elsewhere we have tackled marriage, biblical manhood and womanhood, money, and other hot topics.

Ligon Duncan is senior minister of First Presbyterian Church in Jackson, Mississippi, and coauthor of *Baptism and the Lord's Supper* (Crossway).

21

Matt Chandler

My questions

I am predominately concerned with the text, but when preparation moves to application of the text, I think through the following questions:

- What objections will those who aren't believers (both pagans and those who are the religiously lost) have to this text?

- Has this text been taught incorrectly in recent history?

- How does the application of this text vary to people across the different stages of life—from high school student, college student, single adult, married adult, or empty nester? How does the application vary from a male or female perspective?

- Have I correctly and faithfully pointed people to the person and work of Christ and the gospel in this text?

My process

I have three separate two-and-a-half-hour lockdown study days a week: Tuesdays, Thursdays, and Saturday mornings. I am at least six weeks ahead and can be almost six months ahead at certain times of the year. I usually adhere to the following schedule:

- On Tuesdays I do most of my exegesis and build out sermon outlines.

- On Thursdays I begin to put flesh and blood to the sermon outlines. Illustrations, word pictures, and so on all happen on Thursdays. The questions listed above get asked and answered, and the sermon can have radical shifts on that day.

- Saturday is more about making sure the text has read me. I get up to my study at noon, pray over my message, and pray through the text leading up to our first service at 5:00 p.m.

Matt Chandler is pastor of the Village Church in Highland Village, Texas, and author of *The Explicit Gospel* (Crossway).

Lee Eclov

My process

I'm not very structured in these things, but generally I invest the first two or three hours of preparation in simply pondering the passage. I usually have the text printed in a column on a blank page and use colored pens (or I do the same process in Microsoft OneNote).

I try to grasp the "lay" of the passage, the logic and flow. That seems to me to be more significant in clear understanding than word studies and other microscrutiny, which I also do, sometimes simultaneously, sometimes as a second step. I try to pester the passage, like a little kid with lots of questions. I really invest in trying to understand with crystal clarity why *B* follows *A*, why one thought leads to the next. I ask myself, "If I had verse *A*, would I have guessed right about what comes in verse *B*?" What is counterintuitive about this passage? How does this actually work out in my soul's experience? Why would the author put it this way and not that way? I'm very, very curious about what I think of as the interior life of a passage.

This observational process morphs toward more detailed study. I'm not skilled in Greek and have lost all my Hebrew knowledge, so I have to rely on good tools. I often work through the text using my *Logos* software. I don't look up everything, but the observational process has given me a sense about words, phrases, syntax, and such need extra attention. At this point I also read commentaries. I have a good library, so quite often I'll use three to six commentaries—some more textual, others more pastoral. I'm more dependent on these books with some texts than others.

The process up to this point takes about half of my twelve to fifteen hours of preparation time. The balance goes to writing the sermon. That begins with a process of trying to see the most natural and helpful outline of the passage. Generally the natural structure is the most helpful. But my first outline sometimes changes. Throughout the whole process, I'm toying with words and phrases, trying to find the simplest, but most memorable, way of expressing a point. For some reason, I find it easier to do this process with pen and paper than computer. Gradually I find the outline, with subpoints and illustration ideas. Then I turn to writing the sermon.

I always do a full manuscript, but in an outline structure. It's easier for me to follow when I'm preaching because I can see the structure at a glance. I also find that structure easier to edit. I have a special template set up in Word into which I type all my sermons. When I've finished a draft, I quit and go home. Then early on Sunday mornings, I give it one more going-over, and almost always make significant changes.

Writing a sermon, working with wording and structure, finding illustrations and thinking through strong metaphors, can take hours. I always overwrite and have to find ways to cut.

My sermons are typically long (forty minutes is common), and I wish I could find ways to make them shorter, but that doesn't usually happen. (If I just read the manuscript, I would finish in a little over thirty minutes, but extemporizing adds at least five minutes, usually more.)

My schedule

Well, I wish I'd formed a better habit in this area when I was young and formative, because I don't have a pattern that others should probably emulate. I take Mondays off. Tuesdays almost never involve sermon prep. Sometimes I get rolling on prep on Wednesday, but more often I begin with one to three hours on Thursday. I block out Fridays for study, and though there are always other things to attend to, I do devote most of that day, and often work till 7 p.m. or later. Then I pick up again on Saturday and try to be done by noon. Saturday is also a day when I do counseling, so it is hard to squeeze everything in. I wish I could get a much earlier start so I have more gestation time.

Lee Eclov is pastor of Village Church of Lincolnshire in Lake Forest, Illinois, and author of *Pastoral Graces*.

Mark Buchanan

My questions

I use the text as a base for mutual cross-examination: it interrogates me, and I it. I let the Word pry me for secrets, search me for hidden motives, scour my shadows, sort my muddled thoughts. I let it confront me, debunk me, teach me, bolster me, mess with me.

And I in turn subject it to a good grilling: how, why, where, when, who?

For instance, I recently spoke on the Parable of the Talents (Matt. 25:14–30). One of the questions I brought to the text: what does this have to do with the kingdom of God? This is the beginning place to exegete the passage, because the wider context makes it clear that Jesus tells the parable to teach about what the kingdom is like in its consummation, as it comes into its fullness. This question opened the text for me in a fresh way. It helped me see the parable, not so much as a story about financial stewardship (how I'd used it previously), but as a demonstration of how our theology—how we view the master—shapes our actions and attitudes, and how these then have ultimate consequences. As we see God, so shall we live. If we view God as cheap, hard, mean, that's what we'll mimic. Our theology will become our destiny. A taskmaster theology produces a play-it-safe lifestyle, which then dooms us to a dark, sad, anxious world.

That line of questioning led me to another question: what if the man who buried the talent had instead tried to invest it, but in his efforts lost it all? What would the master do then? And I realized, there's another parable that answers that, and then some. The Parable of the Prodigal Son is about an insolent son (surely more galling than a listless servant) who demands his father's wealth, intentionally squanders it, and returns looking for more, with nothing to show for his wasteful indulgence. And the father not only welcomes him, but gives him more than he could ask or imagine: "Come and share in your father's happiness!" God has more room in his heart for the one who wastes his wealth than for the one who never uses it. Among the vices God detests most is overcaution with his boundless riches.

That then began to work me over. Am I too cautious with God's riches, a millionaire playing the pauper? Am I trying to hide cowardice and laziness beneath a cloak of prudence? Am I, in short, failing to take risks with God's bounty that would grow God's kingdom and delight his heart?

That became the question that drove the whole sermon.

My process

On Saturday afternoon, a week prior to preaching the sermon, I spend time in the process described above, and then I do a rough exegesis of the text. I then read any commentaries that may help. This usually requires two hours.

On Monday morning, at the church, I spend an hour outlining the sermon based on my exegetical and reading notes. I write this longhand in my journal. I spend another hour sifting through my stockpile of sermon illustrations that I've accumulated for twenty-one years and keep in a five-drawer legal filing cabinet. I select ten or so illustrations that could fit the sermon, but usually end up using only one or two, three at most.

On Tuesday morning, I spend two hours writing an introduction to the sermon.

On both Wednesday and Thursday mornings, I spend three hours each writing the sermon. I do this on a computer, single-spaced, in 12-point font. It usually finishes at four to five pages. I am always finished by noon on Thursday. I then put the manuscript away and don't think about it until Saturday night.

On Saturday night, the evening prior to preaching, I read the manuscript twice and make any changes or corrections.

On Sunday morning, I read it once. And then I go for a walk and get it in my guts. I leave the manuscript on my desk and walk up to the pulpit with only a Bible. I preach the sermon twice, and never use notes unless I'm quoting someone.

The total time spent, from mulling the text over to standing up to preach it, is ten to twelve hours.

Mark Buchanan is pastor of New Life Community Baptist Church in Duncan, British Columbia, Canada, and author of *Spiritual Rhythm* (Zondervan).

Bryan Wilkerson

My questions

- What's the purpose of preaching this sermon?

- What do I want people to think, feel, or do as a result?

- How would a seeker hear this? I try to imagine one of my neighbors or a seeker I've spoken with recently sitting in the service.

- What's funny about this? I'm always on the hunt for humor that flows naturally out of the text or theme of the message. Does it bring to mind any funny stories or experiences I've had? Does a truth get comical if taken to an extreme?

- What would happen if this truth were wrongly understood or applied?

- Am I fairly representing a position, belief, or practice I am critiquing? For example, if I were teaching on Islam and my Muslim neighbor was sitting in the front row, would he feel accurately and sensitively represented? It's the same when dealing with homosexuality, abortion, atheism, and so on.

- Is there something here for kids to connect to, such as an application, illustration, or phrase that lets them know the message is for them too?

My process

My preparation begins with an overnight study retreat where I get away with a pile of books, Bible, legal pad, running shoes, and a carton of orange juice. I lay out the next series or season of messages with a text and big idea for each, along with worship suggestions for the creative team.

Most of my sermon work is done the week I'm preaching. I study at home for a few hours on Monday morning, mainly working with the text itself, but also with a couple of commentaries. I'll do free associating of ideas, images, and cultural connections with movie scenes, pop songs, poems. On Monday afternoon I sit for thirty to forty-five minutes with our pastor of worship and arts, and we kick the idea around and brainstorm illustrations and ideas.

Tuesday is my day off. I don't usually do any "hard" preparation, but I'm turning the idea over in my head as I do yard work, exercise, and so on. Lots of creative thoughts happen on Tuesday.

Wednesday is mostly meetings, so I get little studying done, but often my sermon ideas are clarified in our two-hour, creative-team meeting as we finalize the service orders for upcoming Sundays.

On Thursday I have three to four hours of study time that I spend in the commentaries and doing Internet scavenging. Ideally I have a rough, two-page outline by noon.

On Friday I spend six to eight hours manuscripting the sermon, beginning early in the morning and working straight through till early afternoon. Ideally I get three-fourths of the rough draft completed.

On Saturday I finish writing the rough manuscript by breakfast. Then I spend three to six hours over the course of the day, evening, and wee hours editing and refining the manuscript. I send the manuscript off to the media team.

On Sunday I wake up very early for three hours of finalizing, "learning," and marking up the manuscript, which I take into the pulpit for occasional referencing.

Of course, my prayer preparation begins on the retreat and continues daily throughout the writing week.

Bryan Wilkerson is pastor of Grace Chapel in Lexington, Massachusetts.

25

Dave Stone

My questions

I try to determine the main take-away from the text. Then I try to translate that into the best take-away for my audience. As I write my sermon, I attempt to give that central theme plenty of ways to breathe through the sermon. I do that through relevant illustrations, supporting Scriptures, humorous stories, and biblical examples. When I write my conclusion, my goal is to challenge the listener to some type of action. I typically will ask myself the *so what?* question. In other words, in light of what I have just taught, so what? That in turn leads me to the specific challenge I will give.

My process

We try to determine our sermon series several months in advance. At that initial stage, our hope is to have a title, text, and perhaps some direction. Then about one month before the series begins, we have a creative planning team that meets to discuss what creative things we can incorporate into the messages. That may not be something done in the sermon—it might be a song, drama, testimony, or video—but we look for creative ways to supplement and enhance the bottom-line message.

As for the sermon, on Monday morning I meet with the worship and preaching staff, and we talk about the service as it is laid out. I will then share some outline thoughts and invite others to share any ideas for supporting Scriptures. On Tuesday and Wednesday, I try to work on my sermon at least three or more hours each of those days.

By noon on Thursday, I try to have a ten-page manuscript. I then have a working lunch with three other guys on staff who love preaching, and we spend an hour slicing and dicing suggestions. On Friday I continue to add last-minute ideas and edit the manuscript.

On Saturday afternoon I practice it and send it on to our tech crew. After I preach the message in our Saturday night worship service, I will receive voice mail suggestions and encouragement from the same gentlemen who read over the sermon on Thursday. On Sunday morning at Waffle House®, I will continue to refine the message. I will call my changes in to the tech department to modify their slides, and then I will preach the sermon two more times on Sunday.

Dave Stone is pastor of Southeast Christian Church in Louisville, Kentucky, and author of *Refining Your Style* (Group).

Kevin Miller

My questions

- What are the big ideas in the text?

- Am I preaching from a natural unit of Scripture?

- What is this text about? What is it saying about what it's about?

- Why did the original audience need to hear this message?

- What question is this text answering? And what is its answer?

- What does this text say about Jesus? Have I stayed in this text until I met the Lord of this text?

- What is the good news of this text?

- How is this passage supposed to make me feel?

- Who has something at stake?

- Does the text really mean that? "But . . ."

- So what?

- What story is being told in this text? What is our part in that story?

- "Yes, but how?" How do I live out this truth in simple, practical ways?

- What questions will people have that I need to answer?

- Does this text bring any songs to mind?

- What props could be used as illustrations?

- Who could give a testimony as an illustration for this sermon?

- What would Tim Keller do?

- What are the implications of this text (not the same as applications)?

- What reality is the text introducing us to?

- What is God inviting us to?

- Why should people care?

- What are the words that catch the wind?

- Who will be in the audience? "A _____ who . . ."

Kevin Miller is associate pastor with Church of the Resurrection in Wheaton, Illinois, and author of *Surviving Information Overload* (Zondervan).

27

Bryan Loritts

My questions

Key questions for me are, what is the genre of the text; is it a narrative, an epistle, historical? Genre is absolutely huge, and most of us don't realize how much genre affects how we decipher words. Other questions I ask center around authorship, location, context of the text.

My process

Mondays and Tuesdays are research days. This is when I do all my reference work: observations, word studies, consulting parallel passages, reading theologies and commentaries.

Wednesday is outline and rough-draft day. On Thursday I write the final manuscript.

Saturday evening and Sunday morning are devoted to reading and praying over the manuscript and practicing it once.

Bryan Loritts is pastor of Fellowship Memphis in Memphis, Tennessee.

Leith Anderson

My questions

One important question for me is, what would the Bible sound like if it were written today? My job is to take Bible truth and make it as interesting and applicable for today's listeners as for the first listeners.

My process

Every July I write the preaching schedule for the next calendar year. It includes titles, topics, texts, sermon summaries, and creative features for the services (videos, drama, interactive elements; give-aways; and such). A file folder is set up for each of the next year's sermons, where I accumulate ideas, articles, commentaries, and more. When the preparation days come before the preaching weekend, I already have a lot of the work done, and the worship, drama, and creative-arts teams have been working for months in advance to coordinate the entire service.

Leith Anderson is former pastor of Wooddale Church in Eden Prairie, Minnesota, and president of the National Association of Evangelicals (NAE). He is author of *The Jesus Revolution* (Abingdon).

Mark Mitchell

My questions

- What did the original writer want to convey to his readers and why? At this point I want to nail down an exegetical outline and one exegetical statement.

- What timeless truth (big idea) can I derive from that exegetical idea?

- How does that timeless truth apply to today? Be specific!

- What is the vision of God in this passage?

- What is the depravity factor? How does this truth intersect with our fallen nature?

- How does this truth relate to God's redemptive purposes in Christ?

- How will I preach this text? Will it be an inductive or deductive sermon? What will my purpose be?

As you might be able to tell, much of this comes from Haddon Robinson's training. He has been a huge help to me.

My process

Weeks in advance of starting a series, I study the overall book and lay it out according to natural units of thought to be used for preaching. I try to have an idea of what the general theme is of each passage at this point.

I am off on Monday, and Tuesday is full of staff meetings, but I usually get a start on my exegetical work sometime on Tuesday afternoon.

Wednesday morning is set aside for sermon prep. I complete my exegetical work and read exegetical commentaries to check my work.

Thursday morning is set aside for sermon prep. I work on going from text to sermon. I try to nail down my sermon outline, the illustrations I will be using, and sermonic strategy. I sometimes try to read a few other sermons on this passage or a preaching commentary to get the creative juices flowing.

On Friday the whole day is given to sermon writing. I don't even come into the office. I write a complete manuscript that will be printed for the church as a whole and placed on our Web site the following week.

I don't look at the sermon again until Saturday night, when I simply review it and make minor changes.

On Sunday morning I take about two hours to go over my sermon and make any last-minute changes.

Mark Mitchell is pastor of Central Peninsula Church in Foster City, California.

30

Bill White

My questions

In my sermon preparation, I use "a missional hermeneutic"— preparing to preach by looking at the assigned text from a missional perspective. I have six key questions that I ask myself and that we ask our whole preaching team to ask when they come to the text. There are two questions each on the doxological, communal, and missional aspects of preaching, basically the "up, in, and out" of many churches' mission statements.

- Where is Jesus in this text? Where does this passage connect to the life, teaching, death, resurrection, and ascension of Jesus Christ?

- How can people meet him in this message? How can I help the congregation truly experience God through this passage, enabling them to love him more deeply with heart, soul, mind, and strength?

- Who is the story for the week? What has the Spirit been doing in the lives of people in our congregation that lines up with this passage, and what is the best way to tell that story?

- How is God shaping our character? How does God, through this passage, seek to shape the character of our local church community so that individually and corporately we reflect his image more clearly?

- How can I proclaim the kingdom? What is the alternative reality that this passage speaks to, and how can I winsomely announce it to the congregation?

- What do I want hearers to do? Where do we want God's people to go in the foreseeable future in response to the appeal of this message, and what practical means do I need to provide them to get there?

My process

Three to six months ahead of time, I work with a team to dream up the series, and then I go and lightly study the passages, set overall direction for the series, make general outlines for the sermons, and assign messages to the preachers on our team. This requires about eight hours per series.

Two months out, I flesh out the series further for the worship leaders and preachers, troubleshooting tricky passages; I work with the team to plan for additional worship service components—such as Communion, testimonies, videos, and writing music—that may assist in the preaching of the Word. This requires four hours per series.

I pray every day for the preaching of the Word. I do this for a couple of minutes a day, but it is invaluable. I fast one meal a week and pray for the preaching of the Word. I spend that time hungering for God to show up.

I keep my eyes open all week for the answers to the above questions.

On Monday morning I spend an hour looking over my text.

On Tuesday I spend half an hour with my copreacher (we have two English preachers and one Spanish preacher a week) to share thoughts, hammer out an outline, and solve problems.

On Friday morning I spend one to two hours working up what slides I'm going to use, editing testimonies, viewing the work of our video guy.

On Sunday morning I spend two hours figuring out what I'm going to say.

So during the week of the sermon, it comes out to about five hours.

Bill White is outreach pastor at Emmanuel Reformed Church in Paramount, California.